"Long before the Enneagram was a buzzword at parties, church staff retreats, and neighborhood gathering spots, Suzanne Stabile was studying the Enneagram and sharing her insights with others. In *The Journey Toward Wholeness*, perhaps her most ambitious project to date, she wove her love of a good story with her passion for the Enneagram and produced a work that students and practitioners alike will find both readable and challenging. *The Journey Toward Wholeness* moves beyond the traditional topics that fascinate Enneagram enthusiasts—relationships and endless descriptions of our various and predictable personality traits—to explore some of the weightier dynamics of this tool, offering both a hope and a challenge: Are we willing to abandon our habitual ways of showing up in the world to become more fully human as a gift to the world?"

Teresa McBean, executive director of the National Association for Christian Recovery and pastor of Northstar Community

"There are true voices of wisdom in the Enneagram field, and Suzanne Stabile is such a person. In *The Journey Toward Wholeness* she places the Enneagram in its correct context—that of healing, of transformation, and of integrating the different aspects of our psyches. Suzanne brings tremendous experience in working with this material and in seeing what aspects of it truly help others. This wonderful book offers clear and accessible insight into the inner workings of our souls. It gives kind and steady guidance on how we can more consciously cooperate with grace and create more balanced, compassionate, and authentically spiritual lives. I suspect this book will be treasured by Enneagram students for many years to come."

Russ Hudson, author of *The Enneagram: Nine Gateways to Presence* and coauthor of *The Wisdom of the Enneagram*

"*The Journey Toward Wholeness* moves us beyond our common overidentification with Enneagram type by leading us into a greater understanding of who we have the innate capacity to become as a whole and integrated person. Through expanded Enneagram teaching, poignant stories, challenging questions, and relevant best practices, Suzanne Stabile expertly guides us in the truth that life can be wildly complex, but that does not mean it needs to be complicated."

Jerome D. Lubbe, author of *The Brain-Based Enneagram: You Are Not a Number*

"During a time when the popularity of the Enneagram is unprecedented and sound bites are plentiful, the depth of this ancient wisdom is often overlooked. Suzanne Stabile, using her uncommon understanding of the Enneagram coupled with her gift of synchronicity and a deep appreciation for storytelling, offers *The Journey Toward Wholeness*. It will be a treasured companion for those who seek the kind of spiritual transformation that will add both peace and goodness to their own lives and to the world around them."

Richard Rohr, Center for Action and Contemplation

"*The Journey Toward Wholeness* is timely and wise. In these pages, you'll find language that will guide you through the lifelong process of becoming who you were made to be. You'll find hope and next steps so you can keep traveling these liminal times at a graceful pace. This book caused me to feel seen and understood, and also challenged me to go deeper, right here where I am. Suzanne Stabile really spoke to me with this book, and I will be returning to it often."

Morgan Harper Nichols, author of *All Along You Were Blooming* and *Forty Days on Being a Five*

"Suzanne Stabile's book will free you to know that there are endless lanes and numerous ways to live your most expansive life. Like the grandson Suzanne introduces us to, as a One I grew up following all the rules working hard to be good. Whatever our number may be, Suzanne encourages us to focus on changing what we do with what we see about ourselves and others. Then we can enjoy the creativity and experimentation that we will find room for."

Juanita Campbell Rasmus, author of *Learning to Be* and *Forty Days on Being a One*

SUZANNE STABILE

The

JOURNEY TOWARD WHOLENESS

ENNEAGRAM WISDOM
FOR STRESS, BALANCE,
AND TRANSFORMATION

An imprint of InterVarsity Press
Downers Grove, Illinois

InterVarsity Press
P.O. Box 1400, Downers Grove, IL 60515-1426
ivpress.com
email@ivpress.com

InterVarsity Press® is the book-publishing division of InterVarsity Christian Fellowship/USA®, a movement of students and faculty active on campus at hundreds of universities, colleges, and schools of nursing in the United States of America, and a member movement of the International Fellowship of Evangelical Students. For information about local and regional activities, visit intervarsity.org.

While any stories in this book are true, some names and identifying information may have been changed to protect the privacy of individuals.

The publisher cannot verify the accuracy or functionality of website URLs used in this book beyond the date of publication.

Cover design and image composite: David Fassett
Interior design: Daniel van Loon
Images: white moving clouds: © Matt Anderson Photography / Moment / Getty Images
     branch of green leaves: © Pramote Polyamate / Moment / Getty Images
     technology human head: © VICTOR HABBICK VISIONS / Getty Images

ISBN 978-1-5140-0116-5 (print)
ISBN 978-1-5140-0117-2 (digital)

Printed in the United States of America ∞

InterVarsity Press is committed to ecological stewardship and to the conservation of natural resources in all our operations. This book was printed using sustainably sourced paper.

Library of Congress Cataloging-in-Publication Data
A catalog record for this book is available from the Library of Congress.

P	21	20	19	18	17	16	15	14	13	12	11	10	9	8	7	6	5	4	3	2	1
Y	39	38	37	36	35	34	33	32	31	30	29	28	27	26	25	24	23	22	21

FOR GIUSEPPE

because walking beside you teaches me that
every moment is filled with potential for goodness,
and that miracles happen all the time.

FOR SHERYL FULLERTON

without your wisdom, clarity, discipline, humor,
and kindness, and in the absence of our friendship,
this book would not have been written.

and

FOR OUR GRANDCHILDREN

Will, Noah, Sam, Gracie, Elle, Joley, Piper, Jase, and Josephine:
it is my hope that this book will add goodness
to the world you will inherit.

I love you!

*How we choose
and
what we choose
make a difference
in what we become
and in
what the world becomes.*

SAINT BONAVENTURE

CONTENTS

TOWARD A BALANCED LIFE

The journey to happiness involves finding the courage to go down into ourselves and take responsibility for what's there: all of it.

RICHARD ROHR

The first time I taught the full content you encounter in these pages was at a workshop in Dallas during the summer of 2019. In the months leading up to that event, I became fascinated with some reading I'd done on the accelerating pace of change and the effect it was having on all of us. I was particularly concerned with technology, climate change, and the realities of globalization, and how, in each of those realms, what had worked in the past was no longer relevant. Which meant that the present was tumultuous. And the future, unknown.

I had been saying for a while that there was anger and anxiety everywhere, falling on all of us, unbidden and unnamed. It seemed to have no focus; it was everywhere in daily life—in families and churches and politics and workplaces and communities. People in places where I was teaching around the country were talking about an erosion of their sense of security and stability. Things felt more chaotic in my own life than usual, and there was an obvious change in some of the things I'd always been able to count on.

The more I read, the more it sounded like what we were and are experiencing is *liminality*, an existential state that I describe as being "betwixt and between." In other words, it's not where we're going and it's not where we've been. Having taught the wisdom of the Enneagram for twenty-five years, I was certain it could help us navigate such uncertain times. I just needed some space to clarify how it would be helpful and what parts of it I should teach in relation to liminal space.

So on the first evening of that event in Dallas, I confessed to a room of three hundred people that I was feeling a lack of peace, and that answers to my questions felt inadequate. But I had no idea how much uncertainty we would be facing only nine months later when the coronavirus pandemic hit.

Since then, and as I write this, people around the world have experienced the uncertainty of liminality even more acutely and for a prolonged time. We spent months wondering if and when the surges of infection would recede. We waited anxiously for a vaccine, and then just as anxiously sat in our cars in very long lines, waiting to be vaccinated or to receive distributions from food banks, wondering if there would be enough for all of us. Even as infection rates improved, no one knew what the future would hold for any of us and we wondered if we could even hope for a return to "normal."

LIVING IN LIMINAL TIMES

The pandemic era is not the first or last liminal time, but it is ours and it is especially acute. Living life during a betwixt and between season—on the threshold that separates what *was* from what *will be*—is a balancing act that few are prepared for since our usual ways of managing life no longer work.

We don't like it when the world around us seems out of control, but let's face it: control is an illusion. It is my favorite illusion, but that doesn't make it real.

The truth is that nothing new happens as long as we are inside our self-constructed comfort zone. More importantly, nothing creative comes from business as usual. Every moment—even, dare I say, a liminal moment— is full of potential if we have the desire and the courage to walk toward it. And the Enneagram is an extraordinarily helpful tool to help us do that.

While liminal space is challenging, it may paradoxically be the best, if not the only, teachable space. We can no longer locate a single cause for anxiety and discomfort, and we can't fall back on our usual explanations or habits or assumptions. Nor can we discern the meaning of the unrest, anxiety, anger, shame, and *dis*-ease we feel. So we have to seek new ways of seeing and making meaning, of letting the uncertainty teach us.

Everyone responds to the discomfort and stress of a liminal time according to their personality type, often with unfortunate results. If we are risk takers by nature, we are anxious to quickly move forward toward a future of our own making. The move is often hasty and lacks the pieces of the past that have value. If we are risk averse, our nature is to "go back to the way things used to be," unaware that there is no such place and that we will have to find the comfort we seek somewhere along the path that lies before us. For those who are present to but confused about what could be accomplished while on the threshold, doing whatever is right in front of us alleviates our cares and woes, but only momentarily.

FINDING BALANCE

I've been told more than once that it's important to live a balanced life. I've been to workshops where speakers taught how to achieve greater balance. I've read books on the topic. I've heard sermons preached about it, and I've visited monasteries where they're actually pretty good at it, though they might not say they were. As it turns out, living a balanced life is not that easy.

Sometimes when I know something *should* be done, I question whether I'm up to the task and then reach for the nearest excuse. Until about ten years ago, I had pretty much given up on achieving any kind of balance for my life. My excuse was that I'm just not well equipped for a balanced life. But as it turns out, that isn't true.

It isn't true for me, and it isn't true for you either.

In fact, Enneagram wisdom suggests two things: First, the key to living—in liminal time or any time—is balance. Second, we all have exactly what we need to find that balance. And that's what this book is all about.

> Every moment is full of potential if we have the desire and the courage to walk toward it.

Perhaps you've studied the Enneagram enough to know what your motivations are. You may know which of your wings came first, what triad you belong to, and the sin or passion associated with your number. All of that is very helpful. But this book is about the three Centers of Intelligence: *thinking, feeling,* and *doing.* It is generally and universally accepted by the world's philosophies and religions that human beings are born with these three native intelligences. Enneagram wisdom teaches us that these intelligences are simply three different ways of meeting the world.

We all have a different combination of these three qualities: one is dominant, one supports the dominant, and one is repressed. These Centers of Intelligence, as the Enneagram names them, are our natural resources, and if we can learn to use each one for its intended purpose, the result will be a more balanced approach to life.

The nine numbers of the Enneagram are divided among three ways, known as triads. Your triad is determined by your first response when you encounter information or situations—with either feeling, thinking, or doing. That is, when you take in information from the environment, do you respond initially with *What do I feel?*, *What do I think?*, or *What will I do?* It's an intuitive, automatic move and it identifies what is known as your *dominant center.* You don't need to try to change this response, but you do need to understand how it affects what you do next.

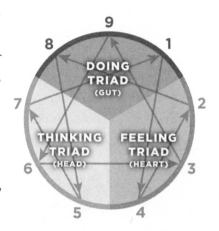

The other two centers are present, but one is supporting the dominant center, and one is repressed or unused. As you'll discover, if you aren't aware that there is more than the dominant center, you end up seeing only one-third of what's happening. And that is the beginning of losing your balance, which will only be exacerbated as you continually try to understand and make sense of your life while using only one of your natural resources.

This is really important because your responses are how you make sense of things, and how you make sense of things determines your worldview. Your worldview determines the choices you make, and your choices have the power to contribute peace and goodness to a world that is in need of both.

TRIADS AND THE DOMINANT
CENTER OF INTELLIGENCE

We'll begin by exploring each of the three triads and the way each number in that triad uses its dominant Center of Intelligence. The challenge we all face is learning to manage our dominant center because if we don't, it will end up managing us.

In all three triads, when the dominant Center of Intelligence is unmanaged, there is a lack of balance. But as you'll see, you can learn to manage your dominant center. There are things you can do to be more aware of its limitations and choices you can make that will help you in learning to use it for its intended purpose.

But first, a caution: you will have no success in an effort to manage your dominant center unless you wrap your arms around the whole of who you are and then do the personal and spiritual work that allows excess feeling, thinking, and doing to fall away. Teresa of Avila, a Spanish Carmelite nun who lived in the Middle Ages, was a theologian of the contemplative life,

> Enneagram wisdom teaches us that the key to living—in liminal times or any time—is balance.

and her words have much to offer to all of us who are on this journey toward wholeness. As she said in her best-known work, *The Interior Castle,* "The feeling remains that God is on the journey." Teresa emphasized the importance of being able to draw near to one's self, all of one's self. In fact, she said, without this embrace of the self, there can be no growth.

Managing Your Dominant Center

The dominant center for Twos, Threes, and Fours is *feeling.* They are all about love, empathy, connection, loss, and pain. But the reality is that emotions are not made, they are allowed. And no emotion is final. For these heart people, anxiety and activity crowd out emotions. And when that happens, emotions can be expressed in unhealthy ways.

The result is often fragmentation in relationships, which is the last thing they want.

The dominant center for Fives, Sixes, and Sevens is *thinking*. They are rational—they choose reasoning over emotions and judgment over reacting. They all struggle with fear, which in Fives is underexpressed, in Sixes is overexpressed, and in Sevens is reframed as a positive. Both feeling and doing for them can be compromised. Their dysfunctional responses to fear limit productive thinking, so they settle instead for lazy thinking, which fails to produce the result they hope for.

The dominant center for Eights, Nines, and Ones is *doing*. People who make up the Doing Center are all somewhat preoccupied with control and less likely to acknowledge feeling or think about what they are doing. They intuitively convert varying emotions into anger, which is why it is sometimes referred to as the Anger Triad—they attempt to manage anger while engaging in activity as a response to the events in their lives. They hold their ground rather than adapt. And they all have some boundary issues.

STANCES AND THE REPRESSED CENTER OF INTELLIGENCE

Although Enneagram *triads* are determined by which of the Centers of Intelligence—thinking, feeling, or doing—is dominant, Enneagram *stances* are determined by which center is repressed. By repressed, I mean underused or ignored. The numbers in the Withdrawing Stance (Fours, Fives, and Nines) repress doing in part because they aren't comfortable connecting with the world. It's not that these numbers don't do anything. The problem is they often don't do what needs to be done.

The numbers in the Aggressive Stance (Threes, Sevens, and Eights) repress feeling. They have an unconscious desire to reshape people and situations. It's not that they don't have feelings and emotions, but they avoid them when they can. And when they can't, they express their feelings indirectly. And the numbers in the Dependent Stance (Ones, Twos, and Sixes) repress thinking. It's not that they don't think—they all would tell you that they think all the time. The question is what they are thinking about. The Thinking Center is underdeveloped in these numbers, so they think nonproductively.

Along with managing your dominant center, the key to wholeness and balance is learning to access and *bring up* your repressed center. In the wisdom of the Enneagram, we bring up our repressed center, the center that we least prefer, when we are able to consciously draw on it. For me as a Two, that has meant learning to balance feeling—my dominant center—with thinking so that I consider more than my emotions in my choices and decisions. I have learned well that living a balanced life will forever be illusive if we don't learn to appropriately use the repressed center.

Be intentional about what is yours to do, and after that let go.

In the second section of the book, we explore each of the three stances and each number in detail. For now, here's a brief overview. The first step toward balance is for each number to accept that their dominant center needs to be managed. The second step is to recognize, and then own, that they are either thinking, feeling, or doing repressed, and then follow that recognition with working to bring up that center. These two steps help us to find more peace and experience less pain, both for ourselves and for those with whom we are in relationship. That's how we begin the work toward achieving balance. It takes effort to choose to do that, but it's well worth it.

THE CHALLENGE OF SOUL WORK

As we commit to this journey, please keep in mind that this is a process. We are making some space for lifelong work, so any thought of reaching a destination is a misunderstanding of the depth of Enneagram wisdom. But along the way, every effort will be met with growth that is worth the work.

Over the years of teaching, leading retreats and workshops, and offering spiritual direction, my husband, Joe, and I have learned that we need to set the table for people to do spiritual work. They can't just come in off the street from the traffic and the noise and the hurry of the world and start reflecting on their lives in a meaningful way. Spiritual leaders have always known that. That's the reason many of the great cathedrals of the world have a labyrinth set into the floor stones in the nave: so all who enter can walk it as a form of meditation, transitioning from the secular to the sacred.

I would encourage you to take time to create a space that can be a home for spiritual practices, including this challenge of deep Enneagram work. Joe and I are blessed with enough room in our home to create a space for prayer and meditation. But when our children were small and we were living in parsonages, we had to settle for a chair. The space is not nearly as important as what you do—and do not do—when you're in it. You might want a small table with a candle and a prayer book of your choosing. Depending on your Enneagram number, you might add a journal and some meaningful objects that represent where you've been and where you hope to go on your journey toward balance and wholeness.

Having some knowledge about your dominant and repressed centers will be very helpful as you try to discern which spiritual practices might be best for you at any point along the way. Your spiritual journey is greatly affected by the spiritual disciplines that you practice. If you choose only disciplines that are based in your dominant center, you lose an opportunity for both growth and balance. It's a challenge to choose disciplines and practices that rely heavily on your repressed center, but that is your growing edge, and it helps orient you toward using the centers in a more balanced way.

Soul work is also best done in the context of community, as we do at the Micah Center, our ministry home in Dallas. We all need companions for the journey because it feels risky to make a commitment to awareness and self-observation. When you add spiritual practices such as centering prayer, journaling, days set apart for solitude or silence, fasting (not just from food), reading authors you don't agree with, volunteer work, and prayer—to mention just a few—it seems hard, ominous, and intimidating. To be sure, you will have to risk being in process, and you will also have to take a chance on being broken in some ways, only to be more enlightened and healed in others. Big things happen one day at a time, and you might miss the nuance of that if you travel alone. It's a courageous journey, so be kind to yourself and your companions, and celebrate every success along the way, no matter how small.

It's my hope that after you read this book, you will want to meet with a friend, or gather with a group of friends, who are committed to doing some deeply personal and potentially transformative work toward wholeness. For that reason, I wrote *The Journey Toward Wholeness Study Guide*, which includes six sessions that offer direction as you try to incorporate what you learn here into your everyday life.

I have one final piece of advice as you begin this book: be intentional about what is yours to do, and after that let go.

Henri Nouwen is one of my spiritual heroes. I'm drawn to him in part because he was a Two, but also because when I read from his work about spiritual growth and faithfulness, I feel like I can do it. Of the many stories he shared with friends and readers, one of my favorites is about his relationship with the Flying Rodleighs. They were a troupe of trapeze artists from South Africa that Henri met in Freiburg, Germany. He wrote that he was "raptured" by their performance. The next day, he returned to see them again, and after the show introduced himself as a great fan.

In the days that followed, they invited him to watch them practice and gave him free tickets. They asked him to dinner and then suggested that he travel with them for a week. He immediately agreed. On that trip, Henri was talking with the leader of the troupe (also named Rodleigh) about flying:

> Rodleigh said, "As a flyer, I must have complete trust in my catcher. The public might think that I am the great star of the trapeze, but the real star is Joe, my catcher. He has to be there for me with split-second precision and grab me out of the air as I come to him on the long jump. The secret," Rodleigh continued, "is that the flyer does nothing and the catcher does everything. When I fly to Joe, I have simply to stretch out my arms and hands and wait for him to catch me and pull me safely over the apron behind the catchbar."

> A flyer must fly, and a catcher must catch, and the flyer must trust, with outstretched arms, that his catcher will be there for him.

The truth about a serious journey under the tutelage of Enneagram wisdom is that you will make changes that lead to transformation. Some of the people in your life will be very happy for you, but others will remind you of the "old you" that they counted on and honestly preferred. As it turns out, people don't love you for your essence, which is your truest self found beneath your personality. They know and love you for your personality.

On the other hand, you will have a chance for moments of loving and honoring yourself from a deep place in your soul that is the very best of you. But you'll never get there if you can't let go, trusting that life will catch you and celebrate with you the gifts of a more balanced way of living your days.

Part One

TRIADS

NAMING AND MANAGING YOUR DOMINANT CENTER OF INTELLIGENCE

HOW WE ARE BROKEN . . . AND HOW WE CAN BE HEALED

A s the spouse of a pastor, one of our realities is that my husband, Joe, has been in the pulpit of the congregation we serve on Sunday mornings, except for rare occasions when we had an opportunity to visit another church for worship. One Sunday, when the children were young, we decided to take one of those days during Black History Month to allow them to experience worship in a predominantly African American church. Saint Luke's United Methodist Church here in Dallas is well known for hospitality, good music, and good preaching, so we decided to join their congregation for Sunday service.

The ushers at Saint Luke's offered us the warmest of greetings, handed us bulletins, and escorted us down to the front row of the sanctuary, declaring that the pastor would be so happy to see Joe and meet the children. BJ, the youngest of our four, was just six years old and, at the time, adjusting to a medication that helped him with being quiet, following rules, and staying focused. We were given the option to medicate on the weekend or not, and we made the choice to medicate on school days only. We were well into the second hour of worship when I ran out of Tic Tacs, pieces of paper for drawing, and patience. BJ had the most wonderful time for the first hour, but then he reached his limit, and I *lasted about twenty more minutes before I reached mine (with BJ, not worship). Joe was pastoring a congregation that had strong feelings about getting to Luby's Cafeteria before the Baptists and, added to that, missing the kickoff for the Dallas Cowboys games was deemed unacceptable. So our children were accustomed to a one-hour worship service.*

As it turns out, my usual options for managing my children are limited when an entire choir is watching and the preacher is either right in front of me, five feet to my right, or five feet to my left. I used up every stern, angry, "you'd better settle down right now or else" look in my repertoire. I was so stressed I could feel the heat in my cheeks and the tension in my neck and shoulders. Joe, who had very little experience worshiping from the pew while surrounded by our children, was no help. He was thoroughly engaged in every aspect of what he later referred to as "one of the best worship experiences he'd ever had."

During the closing hymn I whispered to Joe, "I'm giving BJ his medicine as soon as we get to the car! I'm exhausted! We can skip the weekend next week!" As soon as we got to the car, I told my daughter Jenny to give BJ her water bottle, and I told BJ to lean up so he could take his medicine. The older children and Joe were going on and on about worship when I finally located the pill bottle in the bottom of my bag. Still flustered, I took out two tiny pills and without thinking, put them in my mouth instead of his and swallowed, something the other five family members found hilarious. I'm fairly certain that the dosage was so low that it had little, if any, physical effect for me. But recognizing my own lack of patience with BJ's inability to be patient became a bridge that we crossed to meet one another for many years after that.

OUR RESPONSES TO STRESS

Stress is a reality for all of us for most of our lives. Sometimes stress is brought on by a situation of little consequence, and other times it's the result of a life-changing event. Life may be stressful for minutes, hours, weeks, months, or years. And in every case, it feels terrible and it takes a toll.

It seems that stress is part of life for everyone I know, regardless of age. Living in communities that range from personal to global, we have access to the stories of other people's lives. And whether their stories are my business or not, I find it all stressful.

First graders who need to be quiet and sit still for a long time experience stress. Children who have no one to sit with in the school cafeteria tell me it feels terrible. And middle school seems to be stressful most of the time for everyone involved.

When my children were in their early twenties, they all shared with us from time to time that "adulting" was very stressful. Finding employment, performing well, perhaps losing a position and looking for a new one—all stressful. Finding a home, affording rent or the mortgage, replacing the air conditioner, repairing appliances, maintenance—also stressful.

Other stressors we face at various ages and stages include

- living with family members who are struggling with addiction or who are in recovery.

- aging and everything that goes with it.

- facing health challenges—our own or those of friends or family.

- dealing with rapidly changing technology can be a challenge for some (that's me) because it can make you feel so inadequate.

- understanding our national and local political situations, no matter the political party or beliefs.

Change comes so quickly, and it's inevitable. Many among us struggle to make the necessary adjustments. The list is endless and unique to each of us. There is an equally unending library of material available to tell us how we might mitigate the effects of stress on our bodies and souls. I find it discouraging that, for the most part, we are encouraged to "manage it." That suggests that we can't avoid stress, even though we all want to.

Given the reality that stress is sure to have its place in our lives, we need to take responsibility for naming it and then addressing it in ways that are both healthy and effective. Thankfully, the Enneagram has an ever-deepening wisdom about humanity. As a system, it shows us both how we are broken and how we can be healed. The beauty of the Enneagram is that it can give us tools for being more secure and more at peace in facing stress as we learn to do the inner work of managing our dominant Center of Intelligence—thinking, feeling, or doing—which is the primary way we encounter people or situations in our natural response to the world. Our goal is to develop a structured and organized way of using all three centers, each for its own purpose.

TRIADS AND THE CENTERS OF INTELLIGENCE

The nine numbers of the Enneagram are grouped in triads, each of which shares a dominant Center of Intelligence.

The Feeling Triad: Twos, Threes, and Fours

- In the Feeling (or Heart) Triad, Twos, Threes, and Fours respond to information, events, and people with the question, "What am I feeling?"

- They are fully aware of, and always paying attention to, the needs and agendas of others.

■ They have a significant need for approval and yet they struggle to believe that they are loveable as they are. Their response to life is due, in part, to the fact that they generally search for both love and affirmation outside of themselves.

■ Twos, Threes, and Fours are very familiar with anxiety. In fact, many of them can even tell you how it manifests itself in their bodies. And because they feel "somewhat anxious" most of the time, they often turn other emotions into anxiety.

■ Those who make up the Feeling Triad are pulled to the outer world by focusing on everything outside of themselves. This focus on the outer world results in a desire to control their environment by ordering other people and activities.

■ They like people. They also easily adapt to what they think other people want from them. In fact, sometimes they adapt so easily and so quickly to the feelings of others that they don't have any idea what *they* feel.

The Thinking Triad: Fives, Sixes, and Sevens

■ In the Thinking (or Head) Triad, Fives, Sixes, and Sevens respond to what's happening around them by asking, "What do I think?"

■ Those in this triad want to fully understand everything that interests them. They want to perceive things before acting. And they often work things out in their head—their focus is on their inner world—without ever engaging with others.

- Intelligence and understanding and mental connection are important in this triad, so they find themselves at home in what has been called the information age.

- They like to gather and sort information, perhaps because they are logical and usually very knowledgeable about things and ideas that interest them. Concerned with memory and strategy, they are really talented when it comes to finding where systems overlap.

- These people live their lives by planning. It could even be said that making plans is what makes them happy.

- Fives, Sixes, and Sevens find safety by trying to control or order their inner world. And safety can sometimes be a preoccupation. Hanging out in their heads, so to speak, feels great because they can arrange their perceptions in ways that suit them.

- Someone in the Thinking Triad may be dismissive of a friend in the Feeling Triad whose response appears to be illogical or overly emotional. Managing the dominant center is the key to balancing all three, which is essential to health and wholeness.

The Doing Triad: Eights, Nines, and Ones

- In the Doing (or Gut) Triad, Eights, Nines, and Ones respond to life by asking, "What needs to be done?" (Although that doesn't necessarily mean that they see it as theirs to do.)

- They are focused on accomplishing and pleasure seeking, while making sure to keep themselves safe physically, emotionally, and relationally. The people who make up this triad are usually busy, which suits them because they have lots of vitality and they are very determined, often to the point of being stubborn.

■ Those in the Doing Triad are pulled by both the outer and inner worlds, focusing on one and then the other. They want control over both.

■ They convert varying emotions into anger. Anger may not be pleasant to them, but it is familiar. With some self-observation, they find that they hold their ground, and that they have some boundary issues.

■ Someone in the Doing Triad may have very little patience for someone whose dominant center is thinking because they refuse to move forward without taking time to think things through.

■ Managing doing for this triad means using it intentionally and productively. Otherwise doing will manage them, as they act before they feel or think. And that can potentially negatively influence relationships with others.

THE GIFTS OF YOUR STRESS NUMBER

Within your Enneagram number, if you are self-aware, you can observe patterns of behavior that vary depending on the degree of balance among the three Centers of Intelligence. For example, when Twos in the Feeling Triad don't balance feeling with thinking and doing, they take things personally. As a Two, everything has the potential to feel like it is either about me or because of me when I don't bring up thinking. But when I'm able to balance feeling with thinking and doing, using each center for its purpose, it is clear to me that many of the happenings in my life actually have very little (if anything) to do with me. I've learned to stop and imagine myself as an observer of the scene in order to find my true place in things.

In the absence of prolonged stress, most self-aware people can draw on all three Centers of Intelligence. But when something upsets that balance, they respond by exaggerating their dominant center in an attempt to regain control. When that doesn't work, they do more of the same, which also doesn't work. The solution is to regain balance rather than try to compensate by using more of the same center that is your go to.

One of the gifts of the Enneagram is that each number has a dynamic relationship with four other numbers: the two numbers on either side (wings), as well as the two (stress and security numbers) at the other ends of the arrows in the diagram included here. These four other numbers can be seen as resources that give you access to

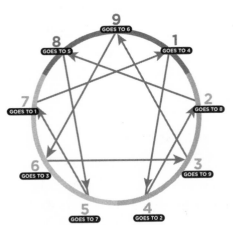

different patterns of behavior. While your core motivation and number never change, your behavior can be influenced by and even make you look like these other numbers.

When we encounter the inevitable stresses of life, whatever their cause, our initial reaction is to exaggerate our normal behavior. In Enneagram thinking, our personality takes over—because our usual way of behaving has worked for us in the past, why not do *more* of it? It's then that our behavior becomes excessive. And when excessive behavior is still unsuccessful, we intuitively draw on the resources of another number in order to feel stronger. That number is our stress number, indicated by the arrow pointing away from your number on the diagram.

After you have correctly identified your Enneagram number—your type—the next most important number for you to understand is the number you move to when you're stressed. The stress number has often been perceived as a negative move. But the reality is you can't take care of yourself without the number you go to in stress.

Sometimes, when we're prayed up and mindful, we find that we do or say just the right thing for the moment at hand. But at other times, when too much is happening or we haven't had enough sleep or we're distracted or sad or afraid or confused or angry, we find that we are slipping. And it's a slippery slope from healthy space in our number to average, and then from average behavior to unhealthy, and maybe on to excess. That place of excess almost always indicates that we are headed for trouble. That's when we intuitively draw on that stress number.

You need to know that drawing on that stress number is a lateral move: it gets you out of the excessive behavior of your number and increases your options, but it doesn't automatically get you to the healthiest aspects of the stress number. A lateral move that takes you to the unhealthy side of the stress number, where you add its regrettable behavior to your number's excessive behavior, is most definitely not helpful.

But after many years of teaching, I have come to believe that the Enneagram is *always* helpful. It makes no sense to me that a system that offers us so much wisdom, and so many options for making better choices that ultimately lead to healthier relationships, would have this one move that makes things worse.

Here's the thing: your instinctual move to your stress number is to its limited and immature way of reacting to people and events. I'm a Two, and I can tell you without hesitation that the move from unhealthy Two to unhealthy Eight doesn't make life any better for me. And it certainly doesn't improve things for those with whom I am in relationship. But a move from unhealthy Two to some of the characteristics of a healthy Eight is one of the primary things that eliminates stress in my life.

Here's why that is true. Twos in general have terrible boundaries. They say yes to things that are not theirs to do, and every yes requires saying no to something else. When I'm aware that I'm beginning to feel stressed and I stop to look at my calendar or examine my priorities, I am usually overwhelmed and somewhat shamed by all that I have committed to and the lack of time to honor those commitments. It has been difficult for me to say no to people since I was a child. However, I've never met an Eight who struggles to say no to things that they either don't want to do or don't think are theirs to do. So, when I'm behaving badly in my own

> The reality is you can't take care of yourself without the number you go to in stress.

number and I am aware enough to choose behavior that I've learned or experienced from the healthy side of Eight, I can say no. That one gift from the number I move to in stress has the potential to keep me from doing things that are not mine to do. And that keeps me from exhaustion, which protects me from excess in my number and keeps me from stress.

As true as that is, it's not entirely simple. Accessing the best resources of our stress number is an enormous help, but only that. It may not resolve the problem because not all problems can be resolved easily. We need to learn to be aware of the many ways we respond to life. And that sounds simple too, but it isn't.

We need to invest ourselves in learning how to access the healthiest, most beneficial resources of the stress number. You don't literally move to that number, and you certainly don't become that number, but you do take on certain behavior patterns of that number. And you act out of those patterns long enough to achieve the self-care you need, to begin relying on your core personality type again. That's why the most important number for you to understand after you have correctly identified your type is the number you move to when you're stressed.

What We Can Learn from Stress

- As a One, you might learn from Four that there are feelings inside of you that don't need fixing.
- As a Two, you might learn from Eight to identify and honor some personal boundaries.
- As a Three, you might learn from Nine that you don't have to make everything happen.
- As a Four, you might learn from Two that giving to others pushes away feelings of fear and abandonment.
- As a Five, you might learn from Seven to move toward others instead of withdrawing and observing.
- As a Six, you might learn from Three that it's possible to move from thinking to doing without making a mistake.
- As a Seven, you might learn from One to complete unfinished projects.
- As an Eight, you might learn from Five to give things a little more thought before making a decision.
- As a Nine, you might learn from Six to use your anxiety as energy for action.

In the following chapters on each number in the triads, you'll find some ideas that will be helpful in avoiding experiences of excess in your number, and you will begin to learn to use the best of the number you access in stress. Keep in mind that you don't become the stress number, nor do you acquire its orientation to time (more on time orientation later) or wings, but with intentional work you acquire its best aspects. It is definitely worth the work. You won't regret whatever you decide to invest.

THE GIFTS OF YOUR SECURITY NUMBER

Just as you draw from one number when stressed, you also draw on the behavior of another number when you're feeling secure—when you're not relying solely on your dominant center. If you're a feeling type, security might mean you're not feeling overwhelmed, your relationships are not problematic, you have enough time to do what you need and want to do, and things are going well.

Look at the Enneagram figure. The move to your security number is indicated by the arrow pointing *toward* your number. For example, Sevens draw from Five behavior when feeling secure, letting go of their need for excess and embracing a "less is more" mentality. All personality types need the behavior available in their security number to experience—and perhaps maintain— holistic healing.

If you're mindful and self-aware and not highly stressed, you can learn how to intentionally employ the qualities and gifts of your security number. You can't snap your fingers and do so on demand,

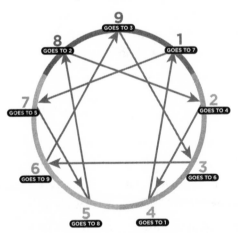

but you can learn to make behavior changes that are effective from that number, one or two at a time, until you have new ways of approaching life that serve you well.

Let me give you an example for Twos who connect to Four in security. Twos are almost always focused outward, and Fours are almost always focused inward. When Fours learn to look outside of themselves more and more, they find that their lives include less stress. And when Twos are secure, when they are able to focus inward, they find that the affirmation they need to feel okay about themselves can actually come from inside.

What We Can Learn from Security

- As a One, you can experience really having fun in Seven. You will get a break from your inner critic, and it will open your heart to your own goodness.

- As a Two, you might learn from Four to focus on your own creative gifts and explore ways of meaningful self-expression.

- As a Three, you might learn from Six that you don't need the spotlight and that you can make significant contributions from behind the scenes.

- As a Four, you might learn from One to pull away from your inner emotional experience in favor of doing more with others for better outcomes.

- As a Five, you might learn from Eight to make decisions with less research and then act on them quickly.

- As a Six, you might learn from Nine to relax into what is, rather than focusing on what could happen but likely will not.

- As a Seven, when you move toward Five you might spend time developing your internal life in a way that ushers you to the depth of something that you find interesting.

- As an Eight, with access to Two you might spend more time filtering decisions through your heart as well as your mind.

- As a Nine, you may realize that in Three you perform more gracefully and that accomplishing comes to you with ease.

Control is an illusion to be sure. We have no way of knowing what each day will bring, what challenges we will face, or whether we will be prepared. But I would suggest that it's possible for us to create an environment for good things to happen. The Enneagram offers wisdom that can help us approach situations in ways that favor a positive outcome. But we have to do the work.

In the chapters that follow we will explore how each of the nine Enneagram numbers can draw on the strengths of their stress numbers, creating the possibility that new choices will become habitual and our ways of living with stress will be less destructive. It will require an honest assessment of your personality, including naming what it looks like when you're healthy and facing what happens when you're in the unhealthy range of your number—which is recognizable as excess in your number. Stress is a predictable part of life. But managing it in a life-giving way can be part of life too.

If we are learning to spend more time in healthy space in our personalities, and if we're successful in finding ways to manage stress that are both appropriate and life-giving, then it seems to me that we will spend more time living out of secure space. And it's when we live out of security that we are able to add goodness and peace and generosity to the world in greater measure. My grandchildren would describe this place of security by saying, "Grams, the juice is definitely worth the squeeze!"

A BETTER WAY

It has become clear to me that few of us realize how many of our responses are habitual, patterned, and predictable. Enneagram wisdom makes us aware of that reality and shows us a better way. Our illusion of control is often just mindless response. But we can't know that until it is named for us and then, moving forward, we can learn to identify and name it for ourselves.

My assistant, Laura, does such good work on behalf of Life in the Trinity Ministry (LTM). One day early in our years of working together, she respectfully said, "When you don't want to do something, would you please stop saying, 'I would love to do that. Just talk to Laura.' That leaves me with the responsibility of telling people no after you tell people yes."

> The most important number for you to understand after you have correctly identified your type is the number you move to when you're stressed.

She was right. Saying "I'd love to" when asked to give a speech or teach at a church is my patterned and predictable response. In fact, it used to be habit. Just habit. It never occurred to me that I was being dishonest. And it certainly didn't dawn on me that I wasn't respecting Laura. Frankly, it's a common Two response. But until I learned the Enneagram, I had no idea.

My hope in sharing this story with you is that it will make a way for you to explore your own predictable, habitual responses to life's circumstances. Once we see what we do, we can be mindful not just about changes that need to be made but also about growth toward transformation and wholeness.

CHAPTER ONE

WHAT DO I FEEL?

THE HEART TRIAD'S RESPONSE TO STRESS

Several years ago, I was driving back to Dallas from teaching at Baylor University in Waco with Luci, who at that time was the executive director at Life in the Trinity Ministry (LTM). Luci is a Three. As a Two, I found the drive home the perfect time for me to feel my feelings and share them. To say that Luci had no interest in reliving anything that happened would be an understatement. She asked a couple of basic questions to ensure that we had handled all the logistics and that the teaching had been well received. It's not that Luci didn't care. It's just that she's always looking to the next thing—she's oriented to the future—and she was already heavily invested in making the next event a success.

At other times, Luci usually listened graciously as we drove, but not that day. As we pulled out of Sonic with our drinks, I was just about to tell her one of my favorite stories from the weekend when I looked over to find her plugging in her phone and telling me that she had a new song she loved and wanted me to hear. As I was about to respond, her music filled the car. As I remember, it was a good song. When it was over, I commented that it was beautiful, and she responded, "Wait till you hear the rest of the playlist. I'm so excited to share it with you."

So, no more reminiscing for me that day. To be honest, my feelings were hurt, but I knew that Luci, as a Three, cared more about the number of people we had in the room, how many were new to an LTM

event, whether they purchased any merchandise, if Baylor would invite
us back, and other metrics of success. It's how Threes see the world. "Good
thing I know the Enneagram," I thought as I settled in for the drive and
listened to the playlist she was so eager to share.

ENGAGING THE WORLD WITH FEELING

The Feeling Triad (also called the Heart Triad or the Emotionally
Centered Triad) is made up of people whose point of reference is
other people. They like people and they want to know how they are
perceived by others. They read others for approval or a lack thereof, and they can seamlessly adapt to what they think others want from them. The life task for those in this triad is to create a world where they are connected to others. In order to do that, they try to craft a self-image that is loveable and desirable and worth keeping.

> The life task for the people in this triad is to create a world where they are connected to others.

The three personality types that make up the Feeling Triad—
Twos, Threes, and Fours—are perhaps more different than they are
the same, with one exception: they all respond to information from
the environment by asking, "What do I feel?" Then they act on
what those feelings tell them to do.

Life pulls them toward the world outside of themselves where
there are people who need them, people to lead, and people to respond to. In their search for security, their unrehearsed response is
to try to control other people and their activities. But for them, as
for all of us, control is short-lived at best.

In exploring this triad, it's important that we all share the same
definitions for emotion and feeling as they are understood in the
context of Enneagram work. Emotions are outward expressions of

internal feelings. Feelings are triggered by external stimuli; emotions come from your mind and possibly your soul. For example, fear is a feeling; anxiety is an emotion. Joy is a feeling; happiness is an emotion. Rage is a feeling; anger is an emotion. Shame is a feeling; guilt is an emotion. Grief is a feeling; sadness is an emotion. Feelings are often temporary, and they subside once the stimulus is no longer present. Emotions will stay with you for years because they are seated in your mind.

Perhaps an example will make this distinction clearer. When my dad went into the hospital to be treated for congestive heart failure, we knew he was near death. When our family gathered at the hospital for a vigil, we all anxiously awaited our chance to be one of the two who could go into ICU during visiting times. I loved him deeply. And each time I was with him, I was grieving. I'd never really felt anything so all encompassing. And I was still grieving at his funeral and burial. After some weeks of grief, I began to dwell more on memories of us together, of him with my children or Joe, and some especially beautiful memories of him with my mom. And during that time of sweet remembering, my grief turned to sadness. Now after thirty-one years, I experience sadness and sometimes sweet melancholy, but there is no more grieving.

Twos, Threes, and Fours change so quickly in response to the feelings of other people that they often can't name their own feelings, much less know what they want or need. Because it's such a struggle at times for them to know or pay attention to their own genuine feelings, they can come across as overly cheerful or overly melancholy, and most of the time neither arises from a genuine, deep feeling. Until these personality types have done some good work, they may imitate what other people feel or they might determine what the environment expects of them by watching others rather than connecting to their own needs and what they feel.

How the Heart Triad Engages with Feelings

Twos externalize feelings. This means that the emotions of Twos are focused outward and usually overexpressed. Twos feel what others feel, rather than feeling their own feelings and needs.

Threes set feelings aside. Threes are the most out of touch with their feelings because they find feelings too unpredictable. Threes are concerned that feelings get in the way of their focus on efficiency and effectiveness. Threes almost always plan to deal with their feelings later, but they seldom do.

Fours internalize feelings. Fours dwell on their feelings. If they are sad, then they want to be sadder. And if happy, they want to be happier. They want to connect to other people emotionally, yet they want to stay disconnected at the same time. Fours are the most complex number on the Enneagram, and this is one place where it is very noticeable. Fours willingly share emotions, which are the external expressions of their feelings. They are less likely to risk sharing their deep and heartfelt feelings unless they feel safe.

In addition to a complex relationship with feelings, people in the Feeling Triad are almost always focused outside of themselves. So, they all either imitate what other people feel or they determine what the environment expects of them by watching others.

Twos, Threes, and Fours seldom claim *fear* or *anger*. If asked whether they're afraid or angry, they respond with something like, "I'm frustrated" or "I'm not sure what's going on." Even though they can't accurately name what they're feeling, they still try to manage it through doing. They might go on a house cleaning binge. Or take on more than they should at work. Or offer to drive someone to a medical appointment. Sometimes, while alone or driving in the car, they may have conversations with the imaginary other to work through the anxiety they feel rising inside of them.

At the deepest level, their heart qualities are the source of their *identity*, but in all their doing to take care of other people, they have lost contact with what that identity is. They don't feel valued and loved, and as a result they feel shame. And shame waits just below the surface, ready at any moment to become part of their identity. In fact, all three numbers are trying to feel valuable by means of their self-image because it's their intuitive way of trying to escape shame. Twos become ultra-good, trying to care for and serve others. Threes try to be perfect in performance and outstanding in achievement. And Fours dramatize losses and hurts, and see themselves as victims.

We could also refer to these personality types as the *Anxiety Triad* because they are anxious about relationships, making plans, setting goals, feeling accomplished, and being understood, to name a few of their concerns. They intuitively convert other emotions into anxiety. Even though anxious feelings are very uncomfortable, they are also familiar. Suzanne Zuercher, a Benedictine nun and wise Enneagram teacher, says, "Emotions are not made, they are allowed into experience; all of the anxious activity of Twos, Threes, and Fours crowds them out." Feeling types need to learn to manage their anxiety so they can respond to what is really happening, as opposed to what they are concerned might happen.

When the numbers in this triad feel stressed, they draw on the energy of their *stress numbers*. On the Enneagram, as indicated by the arrows, this is known as a "move": Twos move to Eight, Threes move to Nine, and Fours move to Two. Those are instinctive default moves that can be lateral—to the average side of their stress number—but these numbers have the potential to be more life-giving if they can learn to access the resources of the healthy or "high side" of that number.

At this point, it should be clear that being in the Feeling Triad doesn't mean that Twos, Threes, and Fours are the best on the Enneagram at dealing with their feelings. In fact, the opposite is true.

SAFEGUARDING THE SOUL

I've known for a long time that much of how we interact with both our local ecology and the much larger global community—how we feel, what we think, and what we do—is shaped by three things:

How we see (our Enneagram number)

How vulnerable we are (our social context)

Our belief in something bigger than ourselves (our faith)

We are constantly affected by the world around us, but unless something unusual is happening we might hardly notice. In his book *Situations Matter*, Sam Sommers says, "To understand human nature, you must appreciate the power of situations." Unfortunately, the pandemic provided us a most unusual and *powerful* situation. Paying attention was no longer optional.

> Even when there is much to do, we must first guard our souls.

I've learned a lot from living during a global pandemic. But there is one piece of wisdom that stands above the rest: even when there is much to do, we must first guard our souls. Of course, guarding our souls looks different for each of us, and the greatest task for those who are in the Feeling Triad is to learn to love themselves.

Keep in mind, Twos, Threes, and Fours look for value and identity by expressing qualities of the heart—remember, feelings are dominant for them—but those qualities are almost always focused *outward*. So when asked how they feel about themselves, their answers reflect their relationships, along with any of their accomplishments that have benefited others. They spend a lot of time reaching out to others and hoping they reach back because it feels right and good.

Additionally, they often rely on the image they have crafted for themselves: *I am helpful,* or *I am successful,* or *I am authentic.* Without some intentionality they will use thinking and doing merely as a means of expressing the image they believe others will see as valuable.

For these types, learning to love themselves includes not only loving others, loving a self-image, or loving the role they occupy. Please don't be dismissive of that last sentence. It is very challenging.

SPIRITUAL PRACTICES
for the FEELING TRIAD

THE FIRST STEP in learning to guard your soul is acknowledging the truth of what you've learned here. Then write an inventory of your own feelings and emotions. You will find them pressed down, but you can uncover them by disregarding, for a day or an afternoon or an hour, what the environment expects of you. Be aware as you do this good work that fulfilling others' expectations provides the approval you seek, but it's a poor substitute for other, more intimate desires.

You are God's beloved. You are loved exactly as you are. If you can find the courage to manage your feelings, you will experience some affection for yourself, some acceptance of your inherent value—even without accolades from others—and some real joy about who you are as a human being. Then you will be ready to practice self-care, whatever that looks like for you. Keep in mind that what you do can only be measured by how it makes you feel.

We all need what the medieval theologian and contemplative Teresa of Avila describes as "an interior castle," a place to return to time and time again so we can remember who and whose we are. It will give us the strength and the character to greet another day. The only thing is—you have to build it yourself.

2s

I CAN SAY NO

'm a Two, and when I walk into a room, I read what is going on with everyone, whether there's a problem, and what needs to be done to address it. If you aren't a Two, it's really hard to understand how we know what we know, and why we can so often be found trying to help make things right in someone else's life.

Years ago, when I hadn't been teaching the Enneagram long, I walked into the room where I would be speaking and noticed a woman sitting in the front row. As I put my bag down by the podium, I felt it. Palpable anger. I turned to the woman and said, "How are you today?"

"Not good," she replied.

"I'm sorry, is there anything I can do?"

"I doubt it. It's been thirty-five years today."

"Thirty-five years?"

"Yes. That's when he left with her. Thirty-five years ago, right now, almost to the minute."

Well. There was no way to fix that.

Knowing she and I would both be mindful of her anger, all I had to offer was the workshop. So then, using my best gathering voice, I said, "Okay everyone, it's time to get started. Good morning!"

And then we went about our day together.

THE TWO WAY OF SEEING THE WORLD

Twos connect to other people by picking up on their feelings, asking themselves the question, "What does the other person want or need?" and then responding by doing something. They seldom question the validity of their perception.

That way of seeing and responding to the world plays out in these other ways as well:

- For Twos, everything is relational. They make their way by connecting with everyone they encounter, and they have the highest social intelligence of all the numbers.

- Twos don't know who they are unless they get that information from someone else.

- Twos are helpers. Even though they are out of touch with their own needs, they have an uncanny ability to read other people, anticipate their needs, and try to meet them. All because they don't think they will be wanted if they aren't needed.

- Twos express emotions easily, but their expressed feelings are seldom their own.

- Twos are afraid to express their own needs or desires because if no one responds to them, they fear they won't be able to manage the pain and disappointment.

- Twos usually believe that their generosity is altruistic and that they are giving for the pleasure it offers both to them and the recipient of their kindness. They usually have no idea that they expect to get something in return.

- Immature Twos (which could be any age) act on impulse, substituting hunches for critical thinking.

- When Twos feel angry it's often because they believe their love for another person and their tireless efforts to care for them have been taken for granted.

- At times Twos give too much of their time and energy to others, leaving little room for those they love the most, which is always followed by shame.

- Many cultures encourage Twoness in women, which means they may never have access to their own needs and desires.

WHEN TWOS ARE STRESSED

When learning about the nine numbers or types, one could easily overlook the connection between passions (or sins) and stress. It would not be correct to say that pride (the Two's passion) is the cause of stress in their lives, but the connection is undeniable. In Twos, pride takes the form of their inability or unwillingness to know and name their own needs because they are so selflessly busy taking care of other people.

It is a tenet of Enneagram wisdom that the best part of you is also the worst part of you. In this case, the Two gift of generosity is lovely. But it can be, and often is, very unhealthy. More often than not, Twos give and give and give until they are empty, and then return to their own lives with very little energy left for taking care of themselves.

The desire of Twos to be *wanted* has few, if any, boundaries. And unfortunately, the measure for being *wanted* is determined by how much they feel *needed*.

Here's what this looks like: when a Two feels other people's feelings, the anxiety of wanting to help that follows then prompts action. So the Two will set up relationships by sensing the needs of another and meeting those needs. It's easy for others to let this pattern develop, knowing that every time they call a Two asking for advice or help with things large or small, the Two steps up. In fact, they must because Twos fear that the relationship will end if they don't or can't step up for a friend.

But then, when a Two's circle of friends is overflowing and each "friend" has expectations that the Two will answer when they call, stop what they're doing to listen, offer just the right advice, and have enough time to assist in some way, the Two soon becomes exhausted, overwhelmed, and resentful.

This results in overwhelming stress: Twos are angry because their needs collide with the many ways they have committed to meeting others' needs. But even as children, they experienced anxiety when their needs were on a collision course with the needs of others. During childhood, they knew they were loved, but they believed that love was conditional: they were loved for being helpful and pleasing—not merely for being. It is very difficult when Twos, who believe they have signed up for a lifelong commitment to the wants, needs, and desires of others, fear that naming their own needs may cost them the connections they value and the affection they crave.

Keep in mind that this stress has mostly been brought on by the Twos themselves. Perhaps because it feels so good to take care of other people, Twos seem to have no sense of how much they are giving or how it affects them physically. Twos unknowingly learn to repress moderate physical pain because they are disconnected from their bodies. When the pain is more severe and it interferes with the ability to do life as they would like, resentment accompanies the regret and shame Twos feel for not taking appropriate care of themselves.

THE MOVE TO EIGHT IN STRESS

When stressed, Twos double down and do more of the very things causing their stress. Tired, angry Twos just give more to more people, with less discernment and much less satisfaction. That behavior is unsustainable, which makes the move to Eight inevitable.

I am convinced that we cannot take care of ourselves without the number we move toward in stress. Twos need to know and understand both the best and the worst of Eights so they can access the most mature behavior when they hit bottom. The question is whether or not the Two will take advantage of the qualities of the high, healthy side of Eight or the low side, where unhealthy Eight behavior combined with unhealthy Two behavior is sure to create more problems than it solves.

On the unhealthy side of Eight, Twos blame other people for their unhappiness. They blow up. They feel empty and angry, but they can't name that, so they complain that they have been taken for granted by people who were only pretending to love them all along. Twos in this place who can find someone to listen often share a litany of all the things they've done for others that were expected but not appreciated. They become demanding and controlling, and those who love and care about them are caught off-guard, unaware of where the aggression is coming from and unsure how to respond effectively.

> Until we become aware of our own feelings and needs, we will continue in the same patterns of doing that lead to stress.

With some practice, Twos can learn to choose healthy Eight behavior when they first begin to feel stressed, and that can make all the difference. Twos who access the healthy side of Eight have more self-confidence and care less about what other people think. They find that they can say no to things that are not theirs to do and they have more patience with process and personal differences.

Keep in mind that Twos have terrible boundaries, in part because their orientation to time is the present. They deal with whoever or whatever is right in front of them, which means they are usually overcommitted because they struggle to say no. They have little, if any, discipline around honoring both their time, their schedules, and their commitments.

Eight energy helps Twos find greater health by first paying attention to what is theirs to do. For me, as a Two, the questions that help me every day are:

Why am I moving toward this other person?

What, if anything, do I expect to get in return?

Does the other person even want my help?

When Twos are able to access some of the higher, healthier qualities of Eight, their boundaries are more obvious. They don't struggle with meeting the demands of the moment. Instead, they continue on with their agenda for the day, believing if something is theirs to do, it will present itself in a much more discernable way.

As a Two, sometimes when I'm at the grocery store and I have very little time, I find myself looking for people who might need my help. It's ridiculous! But in the moment, it is comforting to me. And it is behavior that an Eight would *never* consider. Honestly, I not only grow in my ability to say no to others when I access Eight energy—I am also better at saying no to myself.

THE KEY: BECOME AWARE OF YOUR OWN NEEDS

In Enneagram teaching, balance among the three Centers of Intelligence (meaning to use each one for its intended purpose) will lead to healthier, more holistic lives. Allowing two of the centers to do the work intended for all three centers means Twos are managing our lives at the lowest and most mechanical level when we could be doing so much better.

Twos, whose first question is always *What do I feel?*, can begin to find and maintain that balance by observing themselves as they go through the day. My suggestion for Twos is to watch for feelings and the emotions that follow, and then pay particular attention to the response. In doing so, we are learning to focus inward rather than outward (which is what we usually do). Until we become aware of our own feelings and needs, we will continue in the same patterns of doing that lead to stress.

TRY THIS

PRACTICES FOR TWOS IN MANAGING FEELINGS

- Be aware when your feelings are controlled by other people's needs.
- Learn to know who you are from the inside out and not from the outside in. What is *your own* reaction to a situation?
- Recognize when attention shifts from personal desires and honest feelings to compliance with the feelings of others.
- Commit to fewer relationships and enjoy the ones you have more.
- Set healthy boundaries at the first sign of resentment; ask for what you need and say no when it's appropriate.
- To avoid resentment, learn to limit yourself to what is yours to do rather than figuring out more ways to accommodate others.
- Adopt some practices such as yoga, meditation, or mindful walking that will connect you with your body. Your head will lie to you, and your heart will lie to you, but your body will not. Learn to pay attention to what it tells you.
- Spend time alone. You will have a much better chance of knowing what you want or need if you have time away.
- Awareness is sometimes momentary. Consider keeping a journal as a way of claiming things you learn about yourself so that you can build on the good and allow behavior that doesn't serve you well to fall away.

THE MOVE TO FOUR IN SECURITY

When all seems right with the world, meaning it's as good as it can be and we feel somewhat safe, we have access to some of the predictable behavior of our security number, as indicated by the arrow pointing toward your number on the Enneagram.

For Twos, that number is Four. As a Two, my focus is usually outward, and a Four's focus is almost always inward. In moving toward Four I'm learning to look inside of myself for what I need. Without this move, I can only measure my value and meet my needs from the outside in. That leaves me, along with other Twos, trapped in comparison and competition accompanied by winning and losing. At my age, I have come to see this move as evolutionary because it seems most of us access our security number more as we live longer. Perhaps it's because as we get older, we just naturally find more comfort with ourselves as we are.

For Twos, everything is relational.

When experiencing the gifts of a Four, Twos can use their more inwardly focused attention to examine their own emotional lives. It's a good move toward self-care, something Twos often neglect. They discover some self-worth that isn't connected to helping others. Many Twos have shared with me that they find their own creativity and self-expression when they have access to a Four's way of seeing the world. But I would warn that it's hard for Twos to be focused inward if there is even one other person in the room. We are always at least somewhat aware of the needs and concerns of others because that's how we see the world, so Twos need solitude to do their work.

The melding of Two with Four holds at least one more gift for Twos. From the Four perspective, Twos can name, accept, and even admit their own feelings. Their expressions of those feelings may include anger, loneliness, jealousy, fear, and all of the other possibilities.

The important thing for Twos, which comes from this acceptance, is that they can admit that they don't love everybody. And in a way only Twos can understand, this is very freeing.

3s

I CAN ALLOW FEELINGS

Brian and Laura are both Threes on the Enneagram. When people meet Brian, they discover almost immediately that he has a wonderful sense of humor. He's smart and good looking and charming. Laura is equally charming, sharp, and full of good ideas. I intentionally sat them at the same table at a conference so they might get to know one another better and maybe share some of their thoughts about being Threes. And they did.

At a break, Brian pulled out his phone and shared with Laura an image of a round, colored wheel divided into pie shapes with radiating rings and spokes. He said he used this "feeling wheel" as a way of having a vocabulary for naming his feelings. She was both surprised and curious, so he shared an example using the wheel.

In the segment labeled "joyful," the next ring out had words such as creative, energetic, excited (and others), and then the outer ring had the words fascinating, stimulating, delightful, and more. Brian explained that the wheel helps him be more aware of what he feels so that he can be more present to other people, especially in personal relationships. He confided, one Three to another, that he found it shocking how often he had to look at the wheel to identify his feelings.

THE THREE WAY OF SEEING THE WORLD

Although Threes, along with Twos and Fours, are in the Heart Triad, they differ in one significant way from the other two numbers: they are disconnected from their feelings. In part, that's because they learned early on that feelings were not helpful to them in their drive to be successful. And the unpredictable nature of feelings was of no value to their well-crafted image of optimism and well-being.

Some Threes live their entire lives without recognizing that they have lost a vital connection to their own inner life. Work and activity serve as a natural antidepressant that takes them farther from their feelings. And Threes stay busy so feelings and life can't get to them. In a way, Threes are the embodiment of American culture. Our culture tends to value success and ignore the personal (and social) price so many pay to achieve it.

> The qualities of your heart are the true source of your identity.

Threes are the core number in the Feeling Triad. For core numbers, their Center of Intelligence is both dominant and repressed. In the Feeling Triad, that means Threes respond to their environment by asking, "What do I feel?" but they don't use the Feeling Center to make sense of the information they've received or to determine what they will do next.

Keeping this in mind, here are some other important things to consider about Threes.

- Threes learned at an early age to put their feelings aside and become what people around them expected.

- Threes replace feeling with doing and thinking, and control their environment by doing.

- Unlike Twos, who easily read others' feelings, Threes struggle both with reading others' feelings and with recognizing their own.

- Because Threes are feeling repressed and because they want to be liked and appreciated, they sometimes offer the appearance of feelings they aren't experiencing.

- The desire to win and succeed covers up the Three's desire to be loved.

- Threes are all about efficiency and effectiveness. When they are self-aware, they tell me that they sometimes value efficiency over people's needs. And they confess that they really struggle with inefficiency and laziness in others.

- Threes have selective attention, ignoring what might be negative and paying attention to whatever is positive. Threes can change jobs and change identities without breaking stride. And as long as there is enough activity, negative feelings can be kept at bay.

- Threes are invested in controlling outcome, not people.

- Threes have the ability to become whatever or whoever they believe other people want them to be, then deceive themselves into believing they are the person they morph into to please others.

- Threes are enamored with the future and its possibilities for more success, more achievement, more affirmation. The present is mostly a distraction, and they see no value in looking back.

- Threes are competitive; when they experience failure, they quickly reframe it as a partial victory or blame outside factors or other people.

■ A life that focuses on performance necessarily sacrifices an interior life rooted in intimacy and emotional questioning. Intimacy is challenging for Threes because it requires vulnerability, and vulnerability requires being present and being seen as you are, the good and the bad. This is inordinately threatening for Threes. They certainly desire intimacy, but the thought of experiencing it and then losing it feels too risky.

WHEN THREES ARE STRESSED

When stressed, Threes, like all numbers, begin to behave badly. They are very competitive, often putting other people down in order to feel better about themselves. They brag about their accomplishments, sometimes embellishing their successes. They compare themselves to others and note when they see themselves as the winner. Threes in this space are often desperate to be noticed, calling attention to themselves in whatever ways they can. And because of their trouble accurately reading the feelings and responses of others, they often fool themselves into believing they are being well received when they are not.

The sin or passion of the Three in Enneagram language is deceit. This is different from the cultural definition of *deceit*, which is dishonesty or lying. In Enneagram wisdom, deceit stems from Threes putting too much energy into developing their external image and identity at the expense of their inner selves. They are really good at becoming who others want them to be—and that can be different for every group.

I can only imagine the effort it must take, and the stress it must cause, for Threes to reimagine and re-create themselves for every group they belong to. The environment changes. Friend groups change. Families add members. And there are unexpected circumstances that we all find stressful regardless of Enneagram number. Threes are challenged to maintain whatever image that they are known for in their professional and personal communities. They tell me it is both stressful and exhausting to feel pressure to be the right person, with the right image, for the right reasons, at the right time. All the time.

Unfortunately, all this effort also leads Threes to believe they are loved for their well-crafted image rather than for who they truly are. Deceit occurs when Threes join in believing they are only a compilation of the image they craft and their accomplishments. It's heartbreaking because they are so much more.

THE MOVE TO NINE IN STRESS

In stress, Threes move to Nine, where there is more peace and less need to compete and win. Threes tell me that even a lateral move to the low side of Nine is better than being in unhealthy Three space. On the low side of Nine there is a paralysis of sorts where Threes are unable to accomplish anything. They keep moving but nothing gets done. They struggle to prioritize and make decisions, so the non-essentials are handled but the more important tasks are often ignored. None of this helps deal with the stress they are already experiencing, so it's essential to learn to make the move to the healthy side of Nine.

> A life that focuses on performance necessarily sacrifices an interior life rooted in intimacy and emotional questioning.

The most important lesson from the healthy side of Nine for Threes is that they don't have to make everything happen. With some good inner work, they can slow down and learn that it's better at times to find their place in what is already happening. With this move Threes can be more open to other people and their ideas. They relax a bit, are less competitive, and can focus on other things besides winning. They still want to be successful, but they are willing to do that as part of a larger group, rather than as solo performers. And they can see that success is only part of life.

THE KEY: ALLOW YOUR FEELINGS

Enneagram wisdom teaches us that each of the three Centers of Intelligence have their own purpose. The Feeling Center is for being aware of feelings, yours and others. And it's for acknowledging needs. You can't really do either one using only the Thinking and Doing Centers.

Allowing two of the centers to do the work of three means we are managing our lives at the lowest and most mechanical level, when we could be doing so much better. You will have to do at least these two things in order to claim your feelings. First you will need to *stop*. Feelings have to be allowed into consciousness, and your busyness and multitasking crowd them out. Second, you will have to allow the feelings that get through to affect you in some memorable way. And please give this some thought: the qualities of your heart are the true source of your identity.

TRY THIS

PRACTICES FOR THREES IN MANAGING FEELINGS

■ Cultivate the desire to have access to, name, and claim your personal feelings. Stop postponing them and recognize them in real time.

■ Build some free time into your schedule to allow feelings to surface. Stop doing long enough for personal feelings to find a way into your awareness.

■ Understand that you are not your work. If you receive a compliment, consider that it is personal to you, not to what you produce.

■ Be aware that the image you project doesn't necessarily represent your emotional point of view. Consider whether you may be living out of an image you've used for years without getting in touch with your real emotional preferences.

■ Make time for the spiritual practice of Examen two or three times a day. (The spiritual practice of Examen is a traditional way to encounter God by looking over the major experiences of the day and your responses to them. Then ask: Did my actions move toward God, or did my actions lead away from God?) As you reflect, ask yourself, Are people responding well to me? Are they moving toward or away from me? Am I ignoring different parts of my experience? What emotions did I suppress?

■ Check yourself after experiences that energize you or those that leave you exhausted. Both will be indicators of emotions or feelings.

THE MOVE TO SIX IN SECURITY

With the influence of a Six's way of seeing the world, Threes don't need to be in the spotlight. For the sake of relationships and the community, they're willing to participate in a project over which they have little influence. They would even be part of a project that perhaps has ideological value but is likely to fail. With Six influence, Threes find that they want to be connected to something that is bigger than they are, and they easily value what's best for the group. Perhaps the best outcome for Threes in merging with some Six behavior is that it allows for a heightened awareness of their feelings and the feelings of others. The discipline to pay attention to feelings as they arise and address them if necessary is one of the gifts, in security, that Threes can hold on to. The combination of healthy Three and Six behavior sets the table for the Threes to allow more and control less.

4s

MY FEELINGS . . . AND YOURS

In one of the three-year Apprentice Programs I have offered, the Fours who came found it a place where there was time for them to be seen, known, understood, loved, and appreciated, which is seldom true for them. And they taught the rest of us so much.

Lucy was one of those Fours, and the last time we gathered she spoke what we were all feeling and had no way to articulate when she shared this poem with us. That is the gift that is too often hidden in the poignant way Fours see the world.

Crumbs

by Lucy Strandlund

As a child roaming the yards and small fields of my neighborhood
I would pick the prettiest flowers I saw for my mother,
arriving home with sweaty little posies clutched in my hand.
I would offer you something, too,
but diminutive wildflowers don't travel well.
There is the communion we shared though,
how afterwards Jill had crumbs of croissant in her hair.
She said she had received a blessing
from Joe's hands, shiny with buttery crust,
resting solidly atop her head, not pretending to not leave a mark.

It was visible there, what was invisible on the rest of us,
these crumbs we follow toward each other
as hearts guts minds crack open.
This is what I can offer:
assurance that I am not who I was,
marked as I am by pieces we have given and received.

THE FOUR WAY OF SEEING THE WORLD

Fours are the most complex number on the Enneagram. Their way of seeing is both extreme and more nuanced. They look for the beauty in everything, and where there isn't any, they try to create it. Fours can magnify a glimpse of beauty beyond what the rest of us can imagine.

Fours want to be seen and heard, and perhaps even known. They want to be listened to and really heard. They want time to be in conversation with others, asking and answering questions in the dance of getting to know one another. Fours require a certain degree of intensity because that is how they encounter life.

Here are some other points to keep in mind with Fours:

- For Fours, many moods come and go in a day, swinging from one extreme to another. It all seems to be as confusing for them as it is for those with whom they are in relationship.

- Because Fours are very concerned about being abandoned and not being able to manage their feelings, they may prevent themselves from total emotional commitment.

- Fours get their energy from what is tragic, and they are the only number on the Enneagram that can bear witness to others' pain without having to fix it. Those gifts are unique and needed, to be sure, but they don't translate well into ordinary relationships.

- Fours are comfortable with melancholy, but in our culture that prompts others to say, "Why are you so sad?," or "You seem depressed," or "You need to perk up, it's a beautiful day." But melancholy is a nondualistic way of holding feelings. Fours can feel both content and sad, in a sweet cycling of thought.

- Because relationships are important to Fours, they often plan and practice how they will be with others.

- When presented with new opportunities or in getting to know new people, Fours look for flaws because they don't want to be disappointed or surprised later.

- Fours often sabotage their own success by taking on more than they can handle. They commit to more than they can do and then overidentify with the failure that often follows.

WHEN FOURS ARE STRESSED

As children, Fours begin to believe that there is something fundamentally wrong with them. And they are particularly adept at living into that belief. Rose, one of my Enneagram apprentices, says, "I always feel like I'm either too much or too little." My friend Elizabeth talks about being "right-sized for the room." Their intensity is often puzzling to others.

I have come to believe that, with the exception of children of all numbers who experience childhood trauma, life is more stressful for Fours at a younger age. Due to the high value Fours place on relationships, finding their place in situations is fundamental to their well-being, and it's difficult because of the way they see and respond to their experiences. As a little boy, our son BJ called strangers *friends* and acquaintances *best friends*. He would say, "I want to start fast so I can have fun before it's over."

Fours want people to take time to hear them, see them, and get to know them. But people don't take that kind of time in relating anymore. And that's stressful. Fours way of relating is not well suited for social media. They find it very difficult to value small talk unless it leads to a deeper conversation. Their lives are filled with color and texture and dreams that they believe could become a part of making the world a more meaningful place for everyone. Very little, if any, of that can be shared with authenticity in responding with brevity to questions like, "What do you do?" or "Where are you from?" or "How about those Cowboys?"

> Fours are the only number on the Enneagram that can bear witness to others' pain without having to fix it.

Fours value authenticity—theirs and others'—above all else. We don't live in a time that is suited for that either.

The passion or sin for Fours is envy, and it's the backdrop for much of their stress. Envy and jealousy are different, although most people conflate the two. Jealousy is wanting something someone else has. Envy is more a longing for what is not yours. Fours are not jealous of our possessions; they long for our comfort in the world. They want the apparent ease with which other types move through life and they don't know how to have it. When Fours look at others' way of navigating their experiences, it increases their feeling that they are flawed in some way and their belief that there is nothing they can do about it.

When Fours behave badly in their own number, they become pretentious and act like they deserve more than they have. They may be self-indulgent, giving in to their mood swings, while falling into the trap of believing that their imaginings are true. And when they are really unhealthy in their number, Fours may be inclined to pretend to be unavailable (a.k.a., "play hard to get") in order to see if someone will pursue them. In similar fashion they may use being fragile to see if someone will "save" them.

THE MOVE TO TWO IN STRESS

The stress move for Fours can be very helpful in that Twos, healthy or unhealthy, are focused outward and Fours are almost always focused inward. A lateral move toward Two might mean Fours will begin giving to others as a way of protecting themselves from abandonment while ensuring their importance in the relationship. Or, with the same move, Fours may become excessively dependent on someone with whom they hope to have a lasting relationship.

One of my students shared with me that when he first begins to "really pay attention to another person," he has to decide if he wants to be "vulnerable and therefore needy, or the giver and therefore generous." To this day I'm astonished by the insight that young man was willing to share with me. He had invested so much time imagining being in a relationship that he could see himself in either role. Fours can be givers or takers.

> Let your feelings be what they are.

When Fours are unhealthy in their number, they fear being abandoned. But their response to that fear is counterintuitive: they will push you away when they feel like they love you too much to lose you. And then they will pull you back in if they believe that you don't know how much they love you and want to be with you. Fours expect people to leave them and, as a result, sometimes they do. With the externally focused energy of Twos, Fours can concentrate on another person and their feelings as much as they do on their own. It changes the dynamic and depth of the conversation for the better.

THE KEY: SLOW IT DOWN

Fours have a wide range of emotions that come and go quickly. They tell me they don't know which feeling to choose as they pass by. A Four said, "It's like I can reach out and grab one, but my eyes might as well be closed because sometimes they come so quickly that there is no discernment involved." The key for them in managing feelings is to develop the discipline to slow down and choose one. If they do, they will be blessed with another opportunity to practice the discipline of not speaking or responding or reacting until some time has passed. They will learn to wait—for some kind of shift in themselves or in the environment—and then respond. The result will surely be greater balance and equanimity.

TRY THIS

PRACTICES FOR FOURS IN MANAGING FEELINGS

- Once you have received or chosen or grabbed a feeling or an emotion as it enters into your awareness, stop. Just stop and breathe. Slow everything down.

- To manage your emotional mood swings, you will need to be disciplined in separating emotions from feelings. Learn to name what you feel rather than relying on settling for emotions as external expressions of those feelings.

- Accept the value of ordinary feelings. Much of life happens in ordinary time and space, and you are uniquely gifted to find the beauty there that the rest of us may not see.

- Be careful that in your search for depth and meaning you don't miss the gifts that come in more lighthearted relationships.

- Learn to stay present to the feelings of the moment. That's where relationships are built. Retreating to the past, your orientation to time, or daydreaming about the future separates you from your feelings in real time.

■ Don't feed your sad feelings with music and poetry and art. And don't try to intensify happy feelings. Just let your feelings be what they are and allow the emotions that follow to help you to be present to the moment as it is.

■ Help the people around you to understand that they need to be present with intentional steadiness to your moods rather than reacting or responding to your changing emotions by pulling away.

■ When your feelings are not well managed, you can become self-absorbed. The antidote is leaning in to others so that together you can focus on what's important to *them*.

■ Keep a journal that records your good qualities and the ways you share them with others. You have a lot of personal qualities that are enviable. Naming and owning them will help you with your struggle with envy.

■ Be careful when you are connecting all of your past pain and feelings of rejection. When you do that, you tell yourself a story that isn't true.

THE MOVE TO ONE IN SECURITY

In security, Fours move to One, which is a place of centering for them. It's where ideas and dreams are named and recorded in some way. As they separate from their rich, internal, emotional lives, they engage in producing and accomplishing. They can go out in the world and do things well. In offering the fruit of their imagining, they discover the hunger in the world for their way of seeing. The affirmation that follows offers just enough courage for them to keep dreaming of a world filled with color and texture and truth.

Another advantage that comes with the influence of Ones is that Fours can comfortably have feelings without needing to express them or act on them. Because of their commitment to authenticity, when Fours are nervous, they lead with feelings. Why wouldn't they? From their perspective, in the Feeling Triad, it's the obvious place from which to communicate. But speaking and acting in the absence of discernment is often what causes fragmentation in a Four's relationships. So when Fours are learning to establish and value personal boundaries, the addition of some One behavior is a blessing.

And with the addition of some One behavior, Fours are able to be more attuned to what's happening in the present moment. They are tethered to the past because it's their orientation to time, and they enthusiastically look to the future, imagining what could be, daydreaming, and engaging in fantasies. It requires discipline and intentionality to be present to the ordinary moments that contribute to the routine of an ordinary day. In moments with a One's way of seeing, the present is more interesting than Fours have imagined. Relationships are really important in the life of a Four. And relationships happen in the present moment.

CHAPTER TWO

WHAT DO I THINK?

THE HEAD TRIAD'S RESPONSES TO STRESS

I n the early 1980s Joe and I belonged to a spiritual growth group. Together we read books that focused on spiritual formation, agreed to practice certain disciplines together, and prayed. It was our goal to love one another well while encouraging commitment to spiritual practices. I didn't know the Enneagram then, but looking back I can see that three of the members were from the Thinking Triad (also known as the Head Triad or the Fear Triad).

The Five was at our gatherings primarily as an observer. He appeared to be committed to the work we were doing, but we were never sure. He would ask the rest of us about what we read or how we did with the spiritual practice from the previous week. But if asked about his experience, his answers were vague and impersonal.

The Six in our group was faithful to the work we agreed to do together, but beyond asking questions of the rest of us, seemingly unwilling to participate. I now know that Sixes are usually trying to find a way into a conversation, and that for many Sixes, participation is about honoring a commitment to be present. I wish I'd known that then. I could have invited more participation, which would have been a gift for all of us.

The Seven was physically in the room when we met, but he had seldom read the books and he wasn't particularly interested in our discussions. He said he found the practice of spiritual disciplines intriguing, *but probably not what he was looking for. He was the first to leave the group. I now know that Sevens are intrigued by spiritual formation but at the same time they resist repetitive behavior and the discipline we were trying to commit to as a group.*

I can't imagine an example of any group, formed for any reason, at any given time, that wouldn't benefit from knowing something about the Enneagram and understanding that there are nine ways of seeing.

ENGAGING LIFE WITH THINKING

Fives, Sixes, and Sevens, known as the Thinking Triad, encounter the world and life as a set of problems and potential threats that have to be anticipated and worked out. Since thinking is their dominant center, they use thinking as the way they order their inner world.

Those in this triad respond to everything—people, events, challenges—by perceiving, observing, analyzing, and making plans to deal with whatever seems potentially problematic. They take all of their gathered perceptions about life and people and arrange them in a way that's comforting. They believe if they get it all worked out in their heads, they'll be safe from threats from the outside, safe to figure out where they fit in, and in charge of future possibilities. And they do not feel or respond to experiences before they think about them.

With this focus on thinking, the eyes become key. Those in this triad take in information through their eyes and carry it in their heads much more than they realize, and they are constantly trying to integrate all of that information into what is already there. They seldom have "gut feelings," and have such strong boundaries that they are not tuned in to others. It's almost as if they have a mental filing system where everything has to be labeled and then located in the appropriate place. But in a world where new data comes at us all

How the Head Triad Engages with Thinking

Fives, Sixes, and Sevens have detailed future plans. They go through their days with observation and calculation yet find it hard to make decisions about how to move into the future.

For Fives there is always more information to be gathered and considered.

For Sixes there are no ideas that don't require at least one contingency plan and usually more than one.

For Sevens the joy of planning often outweighs the actual experience. So, moving ahead may be postponed time after time until the planning is no longer entertaining.

the time—in enormous and often overwhelming amounts—trying to take it all in, make sense of it, and then hold it is very stressful.

Thinking dominant people have challenges that are unique to their triad. When taking in information and moving it straight to the Thinking Center, they falsely believe they can get everything worked out in their heads. They arrange their thoughts into an order that represents what life is teaching them, and they prefer doing that in private.

The problem with using thinking to deal with fear is that it paralyzes.

But with the advantage of Enneagram wisdom, that kind of choosing becomes second nature. And they have the freedom to begin to respect and trust their thinking in new ways.

This triad's central preoccupation with fear is the reason it is often called the *Fear Triad*. All three numbers experience fear and anxiety, though not in the same ways. Fives experience fear when they have a lack of knowledge, Sixes when they don't feel secure, and Sevens when they anticipate being trapped in boredom or pain.

When the people in the other two triads experience anxiety, they are motivated to do something that will alleviate it. But for the Thinking Triad, anxiety is part of everyday life. When they feel anxious, they respond immediately by moving into their heads where they can think about what's happening, often dwelling obsessively on the same thoughts. When stressed by the ambient anxiety about what is coming at them, they just think about it more.

We are all exposed to reports of danger much of the time, but those in the Thinking Triad experience the most anxiety about preparing for it, whether small or serious, perceived or real. They intuitively try to use thinking to make themselves feel more secure. Often that takes the form of gathering more information and trying to find validation for their thinking with other like-minded people who don't challenge their assumptions. And for those in this triad, something is only true if it fits in proper relation to the rest of their thinking.

> It is always your option to connect with your soul in ways that enlarge rather than diminish the goodness of who you are.

But this quest to use thinking to feel safe is futile for two reasons. First, because the media and other forces are constantly telling us that the world is a dangerous place: viruses, politics, natural disasters, education, employment, climate change—the list of possible fears is unending. In other words, there's always something else to fuel their anxiety.

The second problem with using thinking to deal with fear is that fear can be paralyzing because Sixes don't trust themselves to respond quickly or appropriately. Thinking is not the same as doing, and thinking can shortchange feeling, but people in this triad don't realize that. They also don't know when they've done enough thinking to act on it. When those in this triad learn to see the limits to that kind of thinking, they can allow themselves to recognize their feelings and find that genuine emotions can give them the energy to turn ideas into action.

Relying heavily on gathering information, followed by more thinking, often means these numbers *hold back* and miss out on opportunities for participation. If they wait too long before sharing their ideas with others, they may feel forgotten or overlooked because while they were working things out in their heads, life and people moved on. But when they do participate and share, all that thinking makes their contributions worthwhile and valued, although they may not always see that. Interestingly, they may also hold back because not being involved protects their privacy. From their perspective, being seen and heard often includes vulnerability that may not be worth the risk.

Thinking types try to avoid being influenced by others. The problem is that leaves them open to being influenced only by their own fear and responses to that fear.

The criteria for *what can be trusted* lies with the individual in this triad, meaning they are the only judge of whether the information fits and is right. Fives, Sixes, and Sevens have to be able to assign meaning to their thoughts. Otherwise, they feel uncomfortable and they lose their grip on the illusion of control. And if they don't trust information, it lessens their trust in themselves. Then they have to validate their ideas by finding others who see things the same way they do.

For types in the Thinking Triad, stress comes from their approach to the information they take in. Sometimes the endless information gathering can lead Fives to feel overloaded and question the reliability of information. *What is worth keeping? What is trustworthy?* And if there's too much uncertainty, then they don't know what to think. Sixes are constantly thinking, worrying about worst cases, and asking, "What if . . . ?" All of which is unproductive. And Sevens experience stress when they cannot reframe negatives into positives. Each number differs in the ways they respond to stress, since each of them goes to a different stress number. Fives go to Seven, Sixes go to Three, and Sevens go to One. As we saw with the Feeling Triad, these are instinctive default moves. They can be lateral—to average behavior—or to the healthy, high side; a move that can be learned.

SAFEGUARDING THE SOUL

In *Situations Matter*, Sam Sommers explores the power of context. From my place in the Feeling Triad and my work with the Enneagram, my primary focus has been that people matter. However, trying to distinguish between nine ways of seeing while living during a global pandemic made me acutely aware of how much situations matter. It's just one reason why I've returned to Sommers's wisdom again and again.

I've taught for years that our Enneagram number is determined by how we see. The way we move around the Enneagram is decided in part by how *and* what we see. And for people in the Thinking Triad, their health will depend on *what they think* about how and what they see.

But for all three of these numbers, it is also determined by the fear that is lurking just below the surface, waiting to be engaged. In his book *What Matters Most*, psychologist James Hollis reminds us that fear is the enemy, and that "fear has crowded you into a diminished corridor of that vast mansion of possibility." If you are in this triad, people trust you. Take a brief inventory, right now, and you will be able to quickly name ten people who count on you and who know you to be trustworthy. Try to avoid the temptation to believe you need more courage. Instead, embrace what you know about faith and then lean in to some of the logical reasons why you can have faith in yourself.

SPIRITUAL PRACTICES
for the THINKING TRIAD

IF YOU ARE IN THIS TRIAD and are committed to doing some good soul work, you will need to make a decision about living with your fear. I would encourage you to take an honest inventory in order to learn how much of your life is actually driven by fear. And then you will have to manage it. If not, it will end up managing you. It is always your option to connect with your soul in ways that enlarge rather than diminish the goodness of who you are.

It's up to you to believe that you are God's beloved child, with whom God is well pleased. You can't think your way there because your head is filled with too many arguments to the contrary. But you can live your way into a new way of thinking. The theologian Paul Tillich teaches us that grace is accepting the fact that we are accepted, despite the fact that we are unacceptable. God is love. That means God cannot *not* love us. Our part is to be aware enough to feel it.

5s

FINDING COMFORT IN THE WORLD

I grew up in a small town of five thousand people in the South Plains of Texas. They were all good at heart, but their views of the world and those outside our community were not always as generous as their care for each other.

The brother of one of my dearest friends from childhood, after living a life away from our community, returned to live on the farm with his family for the final years of his life. He was HIV positive, and that horrible disease ultimately took his life. Our little town wasn't really prepared for him or for the reality of AIDS in the 1980s. They, including our pastor, struggled to know how to respond to him and his family. Because of the lack of education about the illness and the fear of all that was unknown, the pastor was hesitant to visit the family after his death.

My beautiful and courageous mother was a nurse and a Five on the Enneagram. She was beloved in our community for her wisdom and quiet care for other people, and for the way she never judged anyone for their responses. She was also known for her pecan pies, which she always delivered to grieving families after the death of a loved one. As she observed how my friend's death had been treated by our community, she set about to study it and think about what might be done about it. She read all she could in order to understand HIV. She talked to doctors about it and later reported that she prayed about her response every day.

Since it was her nature as a Five to avoid involvement in situations not related to her personally, she worked everything out in her head and then she decided what to do. Several days after my friend's brother died, my mother called the pastor and reminded him that he had volunteered on several occasions to drive her anywhere she needed to go if her driver was unavailable (she was eighty-two at the time). She explained to him that she needed to run an errand that would take about an hour and a half. He graciously agreed to pick her up at the appointed time.

When he came to the door to collect her, my mom asked him to please get the two pecan pies from the kitchen counter and carry them to the car. He put the pies in a box for safe transport and took them out to the car. As they backed out of the driveway, he said to my mom, "Where are we going?"

She told the pastor that she was taking the pies to my friend's family who lived twenty-five miles out in the country. She later told me his discomfort was obvious, as she had anticipated, so on their drive she talked with him about things at the church, complimenting him on what she thought he did well, and keeping the conversation pleasant and neutral.

When they arrived, the pastor got out and opened her door. He tried to hand her the box of pies and said he would wait in the car. She said, "Oh no, I can't possibly carry the box and my purse. I could fall. You will need to come with me." And he did.

THE FIVE WAY OF SEEING THE WORLD

As the most internally focused of the numbers in the Thinking Triad, Fives seek to know as much they can. And they gather all this information in order to protect themselves from an environment they find to be both threatening and unpredictable. When Fives find themselves in situations where they aren't in control, they fall back on their need to perceive or to fully understand as much as they can. In that way, like all of us, they control what they can.

Fives picked up a message in childhood that it's not okay to be comfortable in the world, so they aren't. They stay in their heads to find comfort and intuitively manage fear and solve problems by gathering information and knowledge on their own. However, like all of us, sometimes all of that work involved in managing fear leads them to another conclusion. My mom was as afraid of HIV as others in our community. But in doing what she always did—gathering information and trying to understand—she found the courage to engage with our friends.

Fives hesitate to engage at times because they fear that their personal resources and capacities are limited, and they don't want to be seen as incompetent or incapable. They often withdraw and scale back their activities and needs, believing the cultural story that says we live in a world of scarcity. My friend Brian McLaren says, "What you focus on determines what you miss." When Fives focus on things that are diminishing—energy, money, independence, options, privacy, and other realities that are so very personal—they miss what they have. But when they are able to allow for the ebb and flow of their resources as part of the rhythm of life, they often find themselves feeling sufficiently qualified to follow their hearts. In those moments they are prepared to speak up or lead in matters of personal belief, and they are generous with their knowledge.

Here are some other points to keep in mind about Fives.

■ Fives want to know their place, but at the same time, for them, keeping a safe distance means not getting involved. Fives are independent, and they're the only number on the Enneagram that is capable of true neutrality. That's because involvement is less necessary for them than it is for other numbers.

- Fives fear and hate feeling incompetent or incapable. Avoiding those feelings is part of the reason they continually seek more information.

- When afraid, Fives tend to pull away from connections with others while trying to work out everything in their heads.

- Fives believe time is limited, so they hoard time for their own use. This means that any demand on their time or energy is threatening and draining.

- Fives try to exert control by refusing to react to situations. While other numbers attempt to take charge of the problem or control the other people involved, Fives are content with observing, taking in information, and filing it for future use.

- Like the other numbers in the Fear Triad, they have a hard time making decisions and moving to action. External stresses are paralyzing because they are unexpected; if Fives haven't gathered the knowledge to deal with them, they can't act.

- Fives tend to have problems with social insecurity because they experience the environment as unpredictable and potentially threatening. And they believe other people to be more comfortable in the world than they are.

- Relationships are tricky for Fives because they require time, energy, and emotion. Fives selfishly guard their alone time, while maintaining their independence.

WHEN FIVES ARE STRESSED

When stressed, like all of us, Fives behave badly in their own number. Unfortunately, their world tends to become increasingly smaller as they search for security. They're less concerned about the needs and safety of others because they are overfocused on their own needs.

Keep in mind that Fives live under a cloud of scarcity all the time to one degree or another. And when they're stressed, the idea that there isn't enough only exacerbates their fear. Unfortunately, wrapped in their inability to see that they have enough of whatever is required to meet their needs, they choose excessive privacy as part of the protection plan. Perhaps that is because one of the things they've struggled with since childhood is that their needs are going to be a problem for someone else.

When the scarcity is overwhelming, Fives withdraw more than usual, keeping even their thoughts to themselves. In fact, they are often intentionally stingy with information and respond to questions or comments with one-liners, unwilling to expand on what they've said when asked. In this space they don't just avoid people, they push them away. And they use cynicism and sarcasm recklessly in ways that can damage relationships, sometimes beyond repair.

THE MOVE TO SEVEN IN STRESS

The instinctual move for Fives who are stressed is to Seven. It's a lateral move to the low (or unhealthy) side unless Fives have done the necessary work to access healthier behavior associated with Seven. On the low side of Seven, they become frivolous and are easily distracted. That's disconcerting for Fives because they're usually able to stay focused until tasks are completed. They are still "living in their heads," but for some reason they think about things without paying attention to possible consequences. And they find it very hard to stay connected to thoughts, feelings, responsibilities, and other people.

If they can access the healthy side of Seven, they are much more comfortable in the world. In fact, with the influence of Seven, they become more open, easygoing, and less self-conscious. And perhaps the greatest gift to be found here is that they can focus outside of themselves. Without the influence of Seven, Fives struggle to find their place in what is already happening because they usually don't feel that they know where they fit. Adding some of the confidence and comfort that comes with being a healthy Seven is a way for Fives to experience belonging, which is something they desire but find hard to name.

THE KEY: CHOOSE TO CONNECT

As a first step in managing thinking, Fives need to remember that they cannot choose where, when, and by whom they will be affected. But they can choose how they respond. Employing all the Centers of Intelligence allows a healthier and more vulnerable way of responding. And while Fives might say they have no desire to be vulnerable, the truth is we are all vulnerable at some point in life. Vulnerability can teach two necessary things: the value of being affected by others and the ability to feel and name your own desires. The more Fives practice allowing vulnerability, the less they will have to fear.

This kind of vulnerability can play out in a few other ways. First, because Fives allow thinking to dominate—relying on it to the exclusion of everything else—the challenge is to listen to their bodies. Perceiving is often about engaging their inner observer in a way that allows them to merge what's happening internally with what they're experiencing externally. Because it comes naturally to Fives to retreat from their bodies and into their minds, they use ideas and knowledge for defense. But that means they miss out on other ways of knowing. Intuitive, bodily knowing is valuable because while our heads can lie and our hearts can lie, our bodies will not. Fives who learn to listen to their bodies will have an additional source of knowledge that will serve them well in finding comfort in the world.

Second, Fives' belief that they can manage everything with thinking often means they come up with an independent and internal solution for a problem that requires interdependence and an external solution. But when Fives learn to look outside of themselves to other people, they can have a more satisfying range of experiences.

TRY THIS

PRACTICES FOR FIVES IN MANAGING THINKING

■ Set boundaries around the contentment you feel living alone in your head. For example, set aside time when you have complete privacy, but then the rest of the time be available to others for other activities.

■ Try to be aware when you replace emotions with analysis.

■ Realize that when you wall yourself off so you can't be hurt, you also are walling yourself off from affection, understanding, and love. Consider that the protection may not be worth the cost.

■ It will help if you try not to separate your fear from the circumstances that are causing it. If you isolate your fear to think about it, you won't be able to feel appropriately. Keep your mind and emotions connected.

■ Notice when you want to be recognized without the effort of connecting with others and when you want information about their lives without sharing the stories, struggles, and successes from your own.

■ Try disclosing some of your feelings. It might just bring about some change in your relationships because we bond with one another with the exchange of confidentiality.

■ Practice being spontaneous.

■ Increase your awareness of how you tend to hoard by making a list of the circumstances when you do that (with time, money, information, affection, scheduled plans, rubber bands and twist ties, etc.).

■ Pay attention to whether or not, and when, you own your part in things so you can do what is yours to do.

■ Learn to be mindful of how controlling you tend to be.

THE MOVE TO EIGHT IN SECURITY

The key to security is balance among the Centers of Intelligence. As Fives begin to use feeling and doing along with thinking, each for their intended purpose, they will notice differences almost immediately. They will have richer and more life-giving relationships and won't be as tired or as low in energy because they are not thinking their feelings or thinking about doing but then not doing. That's unproductive and a waste of available energy in all three centers.

Fives tell me that when they are feeling secure, when things are lined up properly and make sense, they feel safe and they can experience life more abundantly, and they begin to trust that they

> When Fives learn to look outside of themselves to other people, they can have a more satisfying range of experiences.

will know what they need to know. When healthy Fives go to Eight, they incorporate their observations of the world by accessing some form of feeling and doing rather than merely filing them away in their heads. Self-confidence gradually increases as they grow in their awareness of sparks of "Eightness" that affect how they see the world and how they respond to it. With some Eight on board, Fives don't feel like they have to know everything before they can act.

When they are employing their three Centers of Intelligence and are secure, Fives know they are able to contribute something worthwhile to and for others, and they are willing to risk it. With balance, their thoughts are finally given expression in action and possibly in leadership. But this good work is impossible until Fives learn to name, understand, and manage their thinking. The more Fives practice allowing vulnerability, the less they will have to fear.

6s

TRUSTING MY EXPERIENCE AND MYSELF

I met Sheryl about ten years ago at a conference in Minneapolis. After a missed connection, she found me and asked if we could talk. I had about thirty minutes, so we looked around the church until we found a suitable place. Unfortunately, the only available space was on a well-worn brown sofa in the youth room that had been a resting place for who knows how many adolescents and their refreshments. After the pleasantries, I told her that I was doing some work around the idea of the third-third of life, and she shared that she wanted to do some teaching about her work with the concept of legacy. I was intrigued, and living as I do as a Two, I suggested that we should teach together at the Micah Center, the home of Life in the Trinity Ministry (LTM) in Dallas. We exchanged contact information, and four days later I received a long email from her, posing about twenty questions in typical Six fashion.

The day Sheryl sent the email, she was in a minor car accident. She said she felt it was the nudge she needed to stop asking questions and accept my invitation to teach for a weekend. Why not?

She developed the format and content with my input, and we planned the conference for a few months later. She flew in from the West Coast on her sixty-second birthday and we had the most wonderful weekend, teaching together and learning from one another while enjoying the participants who joined us.

I'm not sure if at first she was trusting me or her own feelings, but it did seem that the whole event moved her out of thinking and into some feeling space. For a Six, that's intuitive but it's also courageous. That brief conversation on the dilapidated brown sofa turned into a strong working relationship and a lovely friendship.

THE SIX WAY OF SEEING THE WORLD

For Sixes, as a core number, thinking is both dominant and re-pressed. They take in information from their environment through the Thinking Center—and they do a lot of thinking—but it isn't necessarily productive in helping them make sense of things. Sixes constantly question everything, including their own responses, which creates doubt, followed by more questions, followed by more doubt. Here are some other points to keep in mind about Sixes.

- All three types in the Thinking Triad have trouble with anxiety, but because they are the core number, Sixes struggle with it the most. Fives are able to distance themselves from others when they feel anxious. Sevens use a smoke screen of activity to hide from it. But Sixes sometimes resist anxiety and sometimes give in to it.

- Because fear is their passion, Sixes are constantly scanning the environment to detect problems or threats and prepare for them. They are always anticipating worst-case scenarios.

- In childhood Sixes learned to wait and check things out before they took a position, so they overvalue people who act decisively and move ahead, although they also watch people in authority to make sure they do what they say they will do. For Sixes, it's all about trust.

- Sixes push back against quick decisions and often find it necessary to hold their ground.

■ They are prone to join like-minded groups of people. It alleviates the pressure they feel to ask clarifying questions about things they aren't sure about, knowing that questioning on their part is not always well received.

■ When Sixes can't manage their unproductive thinking, they tend to look for an external cause to explain an internal fear or an inability to move to action. That is very hard on relationships.

■ Sixes are more involved in group activities than any other number. They are also the number on the Enneagram that is the most concerned about the common good.

■ Sixes are suspicious of people who reveal too much personal information in conversation because that makes them doubt their sincerity. In turn they protect themselves by withholding information about themselves.

WHEN SIXES ARE STRESSED

In modern Enneagram teaching, Sixes may be phobic or counterphobic in managing their fear. Phobic Sixes like structure that is familiar, and rules instituted by an authority they trust. They are comfortable being part of a larger group and building relationships around common interests. Counterphobic Sixes like to provide security by creating structure and are systematic about creating community where everyone can find a place. They look for security by meeting threats head-on and by conquering their fear. When phobic Sixes are stressed, they don't trust themselves and so look outside of themselves for permission and validation. When those in charge don't seem to be credible or trustworthy, they fall back on their personal belief systems—which might be religious, cultural, or political. Counterphobic Sixes, in contrast, tend to push back

against authority figures who are not already on their side. They
feel like they must assert themselves, at least on occasion, to prove
their independence. While at times Sixes seem to be either phobic
or counterphobic, more often they fall somewhere on a continuum
between the two extremes.

When stressed, because they are too much in their heads and
feeling fearful, most Sixes create more problems than they solve.
How could they not? "What if?" is the one question that plays over and over on a loop in their internal dialogue. So it stands to reason that stressed Sixes are more comfortable with thinking and imagining than with doing.

All three types in this triad have trouble with anxiety, but because they are the core number, Sixes struggle with it the most.

They tend to get lost in their thinking while opportunities
and imperatives for involvement may be evaporating.

With unresolved anxiety and stress, Sixes begin to behave badly
in their own number. They aren't sure how to deal with feeling sad
and panicky, so they may look to past issues to understand their
feelings. Interestingly enough, they are comfortable with not
trusting themselves, but in times of unhealthy stress, they don't
trust other people either. So they find themselves in power struggles
that lead nowhere, and then they find someone else to blame for
all the things that aren't as they should be.

THE MOVE TO THREE IN STRESS

For every number, unless something is life threatening, stress tends
to build on itself and on our response to the discomfort. If we're
able to manage those feelings, which usually involves using all
three Centers of Intelligence, we can avoid falling into more anxiety.

But for most of us, the habitual response is to rely more heavily on our dominant center.

When Sixes rely on more thinking, it becomes unproductive. They tend to give in to anxiety and feelings of insecurity, which often brings about the very consequences they most fear. The Six behavior pattern in stress involves thinking of the worst thing that could happen, given any circumstance that is part of their life at the time, and then making a plan for dealing with it. While that kind of preparedness provides comfort, it wastes time because the safety measures are seldom needed. In this place of excess in their number, if Sixes make a lateral move to Three, they often become workaholics. They do too much, and they do it too quickly. When they're busy, fear falls from their awareness. And sometimes, when they're in excess in their number, Sixes find it necessary to misrepresent themselves to others, usually pretending to be more knowledgeable and more experienced than they are. And then they protect this crafted image by refusing to try anything they don't think they will be successful in doing.

> Productive thinking is always available, but fear keeps you from choosing it.

If they can access the healthy side of Three, Sixes are more certain of themselves, and they take action. It's like they tap into the knowledge and experience that's always there but is usually hidden from their awareness. Sixes, with the help of mature Three behavior, are able to separate from the collective, and they know who they are as unique individuals who are part of the group but not defined by it. They feel good about their accomplishments without much second guessing and they are willing to be acknowledged for their unique contributions to the community. They trust themselves.

THE KEY: LEARN THE LIMITS OF THINKING

It's important for Sixes to remember that while thinking is dominant, it is also repressed. In part, that means they take in information from the world using their senses and then move it straight to their heads where they store all of the other data they receive. Information is not knowledge, and knowledge is not wisdom. So, unless they've done some meaningful personal work, they often don't use thinking effectively to make sense of the information they've taken in. Using the metaphor of labeling and filing to represent what happens to gathered data in their heads, they intuitively set that gathered data aside in the stack labeled "to be filed" when they become stressed. That keeps it from being available for prompt action, and they can't assign it to feelings that arise in response to an experience or person. Sixes, along with Ones and Twos, struggle with thinking productively. They need to observe themselves carefully so they will be aware when their thinking is focused on possible future problems and potential solutions. In that awareness, they discover that many of these imagined future problems never come to fruition and the potential solutions are not needed.

TRY THIS

PRACTICES FOR SIXES IN MANAGING THINKING

- Practice shifting your attention. When something happens, stop and think, "How would another Enneagram number react to this?" Then try reacting in the same way they would. It will help you to ask new questions, which leads to new answers, and all of that leads away from lazy thinking.

- Try trusting other people until they give you a reason not to.

- Pay attention when you are looking for hidden motives in others. Are their motives real or an improbable worst-case scenario?

- Try to stay in contact with other people. You have a tendency to pull back from relationships to protect yourself and then you tell yourself that others have left you.

- Take a break from testing and judging people, from making sure that they do what they said they will do and are following the rules. Sometimes you are equally guilty of not following through with a plan or doing what you should do.

- Practice just going ahead with mindful participation rather than believing that you have to think everything through before you can join an activity.

- Practice accepting compliments and praise from others without suspecting that they are attached to expectations. Trust that they are telling you the truth, not just flattering you.

- Commit to figuring out the difference between fear and curiosity. Curiosity is good for you; fear is a habit.

- Keep a journal listing all of the things you are making contingency plans for. Then once a month go back through your entries and see how many of the plans were actually put to use.

- Consider this: productive thinking is always available, but fear keeps you from choosing it. You're really good in an emergency. You're smart and capable and astute. Other people trust you. Practice trusting yourself.

THE MOVE TO NINE IN SECURITY

In the quest to balance thinking, feeling, and doing, Sixes have to do the additional work of learning to accurately evaluate what's happening in their heads. They have to ask: Is my thinking productive or lazy? Is my anxiety warranted or just a habit? This reality check on their thinking allows them to get more distance from their fearful reactions. They have to resolve their doubts about themselves and others before they can feel safe. And that's exactly what happens when Sixes are in a steady place that allows them to access the security of Nine.

Information is not knowledge, and knowledge is not wisdom.

When healthy Sixes go to Nine, they see things from a much broader view. They are less anxious, which means they don't take themselves and things that are happening around them so seriously. The great gift of this move on the Enneagram is that in this space Sixes can trust their own experience of life. I read once that Sixes with Nine influence look more relaxed than healthy Sixes, and I think it's because they are finally able to stop worrying.

It's not an easy journey, especially in recent times, when there are so many questions and so few answers. But when Sixes can honestly merge with some Nine peacefulness, they experience a necessary independence that is really good for their relationship with themselves and others. They attain not only security but also along with it the ability to trust other people. A Six on the healthy side of Nine can believe that everything is going to be all right, and once they experience that kind of security, they want to return to it again and again.

7s

I CAN CHOOSE TO BE SATISFIED

I learn a lot from my guests on my Enneagram Journey *podcast, and I occasionally have the opportunity to host a conversation between two people of the same number. Two Sevens is a lot to handle, but in that environment I find out so much about how they see the world—much more than I would with just one of them.*

About a year ago, Joel, our oldest son and the producer of the podcast, and LeeAnn, one of my former apprentices, both Sevens, were talking about holidays, and I had a chance to listen in.

LeeAnn: "Hey Joel, do you remember holidays the same way other family members do?"

Joel: "What do you mean?"

LeeAnn: "Well, when my family got together for Christmas they were talking about Thanksgiving and our time together, and I didn't recognize anything they were saying. They must have been talking about something I didn't like or found to be intolerably boring. It was like I wasn't even there at Thanksgiving. But I was!"

LeeAnn continued: "I think I have it figured out. I think we Sevens reframe everything in real time, while it's happening. When something is going on around me that I find both unbelievable and potentially painful, I reframe it to suit what I think should be happening or what I want to be a part of. And evidently what I remember is my reframing, not what really happened."

THE SEVEN WAY OF SEEING THE WORLD

It's difficult for Sevens to learn life lessons when opportunities to understand their appropriate place in things are masked by their innate ability to see things the way they want them to be instead of the way they are. And that's often followed by their disinterest or inability to see and own their part in things that don't go well. Sevens move away from pain and toward pleasure, and then they selectively remember the best. Sevens often avoid their anxiety by making future plans that can take precedence over what's happening in real time.

Here are some other things to keep in mind about Sevens:

- When Sevens wake up in the morning, their days are full of possibility. They stay upbeat, working at something until just before they grow weary or run out of energy. At that precise moment they switch to something else before shoulds or boredom set in. And when activity doesn't yield the promise they anticipate and Sevens experience something they can't reframe, stress falls over them like a pall.

- Although they are often charming and appear to be unafraid and at ease with life as it is, Sevens are in the Fear Triad. Sevens diffuse their fear by dialing in to a place of limitless possibility and imagination. For average Sevens there is fear in going too deeply into any one thing. They are great at multitasking and handling constant activity.

- Sevens know they're fearful, and if asked they could tell you why, but they wouldn't want to discuss it.

- In childhood, Sevens came to believe that it's not okay to depend on anyone for anything. They believe they're on their own.

- Sevens don't just go with the flow; they attach themselves to what they find stimulating.

■ Sevens keep their options open, so changing course is effortless.

■ Sevens are fun to be with and they can make things happen, although at times they may not stick around to see things through.

■ On a continuum of emotion ranging from happy to sad, Sevens try to live their lives on the happy side, and it works much of the time, until sadness is unavoidable. They can reframe almost any negative into a positive, and if that doesn't work, they use charm as their second line of defense. And that usually works—until it doesn't.

WHEN SEVENS ARE STRESSED

Stress is paralyzing for Sevens until they find a way to get through it or go around it. Unless they've done some work, they choose to ignore whatever is stressing them. That seldom makes things better, so they begin the slide from average to unhealthy behavior, grabbing onto possibilities as they go, delaying the inevitable as long as they can. During this time, they don't always see other people clearly because their own concerns are the center of their attention while they search for ideas or opportunities that are interesting and stimulating. Sevens are increasingly bored with what they would call the mundane parts of life, and they become intolerant of criticism. When behaving badly in their number, they want their needs and desires to be met immediately. They're impulsive and they can't hold or manage pain. And then they resort to more frenetic activity.

I asked a group of Sevens at an Enneagram event where I was speaking to tell me about their responses to stress. Here's what they said:

"Unless a situation is really serious my motto is, 'Deny everything and keep moving.'"

"In four and a half years, I lost my father, my aunt, my grand-
mother, and my husband. I never put all these losses together.
Instead, I just kept moving, believing everything was fine."

"I dealt with stress with drugs and alcohol."

"I will do anything to get away from the intensity of a stressful
situation."

None of these people felt good about their answers, but they all
shared that it was taking serious work for them to learn to respond
any differently.

THE MOVE TO ONE IN STRESS

The move to One, the Seven stress number, will be lateral unless
they have done the work to learn enough about Ones to choose the
high, healthy side. The combination of unhealthy Seven with average to unhealthy One leaves Sevens taking themselves much too se-
riously. They become hy-percritical of others and very judgmental. They are hindered by dualistic thinking, believing others are either friends or en-emies, right or wrong.

> When Sevens are doing some good work with awareness and self-reflection, and when they're on a journey toward transformation, they can be as committed to silence and solitude as they are to multitasking and activity.

Any kind of both/and thinking is lost. From that position Sevens
insist on their own expertise, which leaves very little room for
others to find their place.

On the healthy side of One, Sevens are able to follow through
with plans. They often tackle unfinished projects and see them
through to completion. There's a dramatic change in this good

space where Sevens are more concerned with quality than quantity. It's also a significant step away from the idea that if two of anything is good, five would be better. It seems that healthy One energy helps Sevens slow down so they can be more centered, making better decisions for themselves and on behalf of others. When Sevens are influenced by good One behavior, clarity emerges from chaos, and accomplishment takes precedence over their normal preoccupation with process. In this calm, thoughtful space, Sevens are much less selfish, and they demonstrate more compassion and concern for others.

THE KEY: ACCEPT SOME LIMITS

To deal with their struggles and their anxiety, Sevens develop a pattern of relying on two Centers of Intelligence—thinking and doing—as protection from their feelings. They are the opposite of Fives in that a Seven's fear is about their ability to cope with their inner world where grief and loss and anxiety are hidden. The more anxious they are, the more pain they repress, and the more they do to avoid the effect of the pain. The result is less satisfaction from their experiences.

When Sevens are doing some good work with awareness and self-reflection, and when they're on a journey toward transformation, they can be as committed to silence and solitude as they are to multitasking and activity. The challenge for them is trying find some balance between the two so they can learn to fill a day or a week with both, instead of struggling to avoid the temptation to be all in for one or the other. Honestly, one of the biggest challenges they face in working toward balance is that those they work with, along with those who are closest to them, prefer the upbeat, full of energy, happy-go-lucky Seven to a more contemplative, quieter, less entertaining version of themselves.

When Sevens realize they can benefit from more balance in their lives, they have to admit to themselves that they are less evolved than their ego has led them to believe. It's actually intuitive for Sevens to have a positive attitude in most things, including how they see themselves, but it's also limited. Once they're able to see themselves objectively, they know that they will have to set some limits if they are to live into the fullness of all that life has to offer.

TRY THIS

PRACTICES FOR SEVENS IN MANAGING THINKING

- It's okay to be more serious and stable. Embrace maturity and age.

- Be aware of your potential for skating on the surface of things. The depth you miss is where the goodies are; if you go there, you will find it very satisfying.

- All good spiritual work involves awareness and self-reflection. You have a tendency to lack balance here— you're often either too hard on yourself or not challenging enough. There's a difference between criticism and honest self-evaluation.

- Keep in mind that you are in the Fear Triad, so you sometimes substitute an idea of what pain is like for the tension of living through the real thing. The latter offers you strength. Your imagination offers very little in relation to experiencing the pain and the deep fear that comes with it.

- Recognize that because you are so charming, you have always gotten away with a lot. Unfortunately, the lesson you learn is that you are entitled to some kind of special treatment.

- Notice when you feel angry because what you think or believe is being questioned, or when you tend to doubt your own self-worth. When you're insecure about your value as a human being, you fall into old patterns of behavior that include stubbornness, dualistic thinking, and questioning whether or not you're ever right. Of course, you are!

■ Practice staying connected to people or conversations instead of tuning out or leaving. Wait until there is a shift either in how you see things or in the environment. See if you can relax into a rhythm that doesn't feel restrictive or boring.

■ Commit to using thinking for its express purpose, not as a substitute for doing or feeling.

THE MOVE TO FIVE IN SECURITY

When Sevens are healthy, they can experience the combination of the best of their number and the goodness of Five space. Sevens usually enter a conversation with humor and then, after some time, gradually begin to show and share some of their deeper understanding and vulnerability. In the secure space of Five, they can omit the humor and be present to others in a less guarded way.

Sevens acknowledge that they are guilty of skating on the surface of things at times. In Five, they develop an inner life where going inward takes them deeper into any subject

> Stress is paralyzing for Sevens until they find a way to get through it or go around it.

or activity. They discover an inner peace that allows them to live with more security and integration, rather than being attracted to an array of possibilities that become distractions. And when they're focused and intent on becoming more knowledgeable about what interests them, they're surprised at their capacity for success in new endeavors.

In Five, Sevens find that they are less opinionated and more thoughtful. They can name their fears and overcome the belief that they're on their own. And then, following that realization, they can be an even greater gift in relationships with the people they love.

CHAPTER THREE

WHAT NEEDS
TO BE DONE?

THE GUT TRIAD'S RESPONSES TO STRESS

O ur daughter Joey is an Eight on the Enneagram and her husband, Billy, is a Nine. Several years ago, they were running errands at a Target with their two boys. The parking lot was crowded, but the aisles were wide, with room enough to pass if you wanted to drive around another car. As they looked for a parking place that could accommodate their large SUV, an altercation developed between a car in front of theirs and a car coming toward them from the opposite direction. It seemed both drivers wanted the same parking place and a game of chicken ensued.

Joey turned to Billy while holding her hand on her belly and said, "Do you feel that?" Billy nodded. (It's normal for Gut Triad people to read the world based on what they feel in their bellies.) Joey laughed, "This is great! Who do you think will win?" Billy was somewhat surprised that she was entertained. It makes him anxious just to watch the confrontation.

As an Eight, Joey represents the exteriorized version of anger; in this case, she found it energizing. Billy as a Nine prefers not to have anything to do with conflict or anything that could steal his peace.

I'm pretty sure neither of their boys is an Enneagram One, but if Ones had been in the car, they would have interiorized their anger,

perhaps feeling complicit for choosing a day when the store was sure to
be crowded and then angry with the drivers of the other cars for causing
a problem.

ENGAGING THE WORLD WITH DOING

Eights, Nines, and Ones, whose dominant center is doing, look at the world and see what needs to be done. However, each one responds differently to what they see. When they each enter a room, any room—at home, at work, everywhere—they instinctively "read" it, looking for hidden agendas and potential conflicts (which is why the triad is sometimes also called the Intuitive Triad).

But reading a room looks different for each type: Eights look to see who is in charge and assess whether or not they can handle it. Nines look for a place where they fit, and with whom, and they avoid any individual who puts out vibes that are angry or have the potential for conflict. Ones look for what's wrong. If others are angry or notably unhappy, they pick it up in their belly before anyone else articulates what's going on. (That's why the triad is sometimes referred to as the Gut or Body Triad.) Eights are energized by conflict and want to get in it. Nines hope it doesn't involve them. And Ones resent it. But if all three are confident about their sense of who they are with and what might come up, they can relax in groups where they feel harmony and trust.

Eights, Nines, and Ones learned early in life that they can get the attention they desire and get what they need by being persistent. Essentially, they make people deal with them, sometimes directly and at other times in more nuanced and indirect ways. They may slow down when people want them to hurry or they may refuse expectations from parents, coworkers, or partners. They tend to disappear when they're feeling mistreated or misunderstood. It all has to do with taking charge of their lives and hiding their

How the Gut Triad Engages with Doing

Eights, Nines, and Ones struggle with "Who am I?" in part because of their confusion about appropriate boundaries and because they take on too much. Even when they are mindful, their personal boundaries often disappear.

Eights don't know when to stand down and listen, or when to stand aside and let others lead.

Nines manage their fear of conflict and disconnection by merging with those around them who are more dominant.

Ones not only do their part in work or other situations, but also take on things that are others' responsibility.

While taking on too much is satisfying for Eights, and merging is a comfortable solution for Nines, Ones resent how much they're doing, and that resentment is intensified by their feeling that it is their duty to "improve" others' work too.

personal vulnerability, which they believe, if exposed, would give others an advantage.

For those in this triad, *anger* is their underlying emotion, waiting to be triggered, felt, or feared, which is why it is also known as the Anger Triad. In fact, their tendency to convert all emotion into anger creates issues for them. Their anger leads them to hold their ground rather than adapt, and they struggle to know where they end and where others begin. While anger is familiar, other unfamiliar emotions cause discomfort and feel threatening in ways that are hard to name.

Anger is not always overt; it may be just under the surface, with a different expression in each number. If an Eight is angry, people know it. But once their anger has been expressed and at least heard, if not received, by the other person, then it's over. Nine anger is passive-aggressive. It is indirect and yet it lands on the right person at the appropriate time. And Ones convert anger into resentment toward themselves or others. If you are the target of a One's anger, you don't forget its harshness.

Another thing about anger for this triad: each of these numbers experiences a strange attraction to intensity when someone is angry with them and when they observe aggressive exchanges between others. Some tell me that the intensity of attraction they feel at times is what frightens them the most.

> Eights, Nines, and Ones struggle with "Who am I?" in part because of their confusion about appropriate boundaries and because they take on too much.

When compared to the way the other two triads respond to a stimulus from the environment, the Doing Triad is the most complicated.

Fives, Sixes, and Sevens are trying to order their *inner* world, so they pull in and move information to their heads to get things straight before moving into action.

Twos, Threes, and Fours are focused on ordering the *outer* world, so their attention is outside of themselves.

Eights, Nines, and Ones find that their energy is pulled *both* ways, from inner to outer and back again. They struggle for control over both. These personality types want to be seen as strong, so they try to be decisive in relationships. Showing weakness makes them feel too vulnerable, so they've learned to respond by hiding their emotions, especially anxiety and fear.

Because sometimes life feels like a battleground for these personality types, they are very concerned with power, integrity, and justice: they are aware of and angered by abuses of power; they like to know who has power so they can watch them, making sure that those who are marginalized are treated fairly; and they are quick to act on behalf of anyone they perceive as an underdog, and to involve themselves in struggles they see as worthwhile.

When things don't go well, these numbers tend to blame themselves, at least internally. They don't always admit that because they're almost always avoiding feelings they can't control. While they appear to be self-confident and strong, inwardly they struggle with some self-doubt. Nines often lose strength because of their fear of fragmentation and disconnection in relationships. Ones are usually locked in a never-ending battle with their inner critic. And Eights are expecting—and at the same time afraid of—betrayal from others, which leaves them doubting themselves while questioning the loyalty of the people in their sphere.

SAFEGUARDING THE SOUL

In *Situations Matter*, Sam Sommers highlights the surprising extent to which we as human beings are influenced by external factors. The world around us is always shaping us, whether we like to admit it or not. And for those in the Doing Triad, their behavior often responds to external influence because they read the world using their gut instincts.

> Admit that though you usually lead with messages of power and strength, there are times when feelings of weakness and vulnerability are not far behind.

Living during a global pandemic changed the pattern of our lives regardless of where we lived and affected the ordinary predictability of how we were living. And whether we liked what we were doing before the pandemic, it was at least familiar, and we longed for it to return. Like almost everyone, I was in a posture of learning, with new questions to ask and answer about Enneagram wisdom. But during that long and difficult time, everyone I know was also trying to find a way to offer something to the greater community for the good of us all.

Eights, Nines, and Ones were in a unique position during the pandemic because their dominant Center of Intelligence is doing. And more than anything else, our doing was affected during that season. Some had to do more than they could manage, others were limited in what they could do to the detriment of their health, and still others didn't know what to do. In addition, isolation was a big part of living during a pandemic, and that compromised these three Enneagram numbers' reliance on being influenced by the ideas, thoughts, and behavior of other people.

SPIRITUAL PRACTICES
for the DOING TRIAD

IF YOU ARE IN THIS TRIAD, consider these suggestions:

First, admit that though you usually lead with messages of power and strength, there are times when feelings of weakness and vulnerability are not far behind.

Second, be honest with yourself about the fact that you consistently hide vulnerabilities that you fear would give others an advantage.

Finally, acknowledge that having your freedom taken away feels like dying.

If these points ring true, they may summarize why it is so difficult and stressful for you in this triad at this time. They also highlight how imperative it is to guard your soul. One of the best things you can do is to engage your doing, in whatever ways you can, in intentional and life-giving ways.

John Wesley, the founder of Methodism (and I think it likely that he was at home in this triad), wisely said, "Do all the good you can, by all the means you can, in all the ways you can, in all the places you can, at all the times you can, to all the people you can." If you develop this orientation to doing now, you can carry it into the future. This way of life was transformational for him. May the same be true for you.

8s

I CAN SLOW DOWN

Joe and I treasure our friendship with author and pastor Nadia Bolz-Weber. We've known one another for more than a decade now, and in those years, we've spent time together, in person and over the phone, when we have been sad, happy, angry, scared, grieving, celebrating, worrying, and more. I've learned a lot about Eights as I have watched and listened to Nadia.

She graciously agreed to be on the Enneagram Journey, *my podcast,* as she was turning fifty. Birthdays are hard for most female Eights, but they also bring an opportunity for reflection that Eights seldom slow down for. In the years preceding that birthday, Nadia had generously shared stories about some significant changes in her life. So with that as the background, I asked her what the Enneagram was teaching her at fifty.

"Oh Suz," she said, "the Enneagram is showing me the destruction in the wake of my Eightness." Her response was soft and vulnerable, yet still strong and decisive. She seemed somewhat surprised by the discovery, as any Eight would be, because Eights don't intentionally hurt anyone. In fact, they have no sense of their effect on others. A discovery like Nadia's requires humility and self-reflection and courage. And it's worth it because it's so transformative.

THE EIGHT WAY OF SEEING THE WORLD

Eights like Nadia have more energy than any other number. And while they are drawn to energy in other people, very few Eights ask themselves how others experience them, so they are often unaware of their impact. Their orientation to the future can make them oblivious to others, and they focus on getting things done, regardless of the potential destruction in their wake. An Eight's first response to any event is always, "What am I going to do?" (not "What do I think?" or "What do I feel?").

Keep in mind these other things about Eights:

- Eights tend to see things in extremes—either-or, right-wrong, friend-foe—and they evaluate their environment to identify who is in charge. If no one seems to be, then they will fill the void themselves, often regardless of age difference or title.

- Eights have a strong dislike for being controlled. They are committed to defining the game so they aren't defined by it.

- Eights try to keep from being affected by their environment by dominating it. As the most openly aggressive of all the numbers, they want to use their energy and self-confidence to have an impact on the world. And they do.

- Eights avoid vulnerability to protect themselves emotionally. They have been told so often that they are too much, too aggressive, that they feel they have to defend themselves by being strong and decisive and avoiding weakness and subordination.

- Eights have difficulty sharing softer, more tender feelings because vocalizing these feelings make them feel weak and often elicits an attempt to escape vulnerability.

- Eights don't like hidden messages or indecisiveness, and cannot suffer passive aggressiveness.

- Eights respect others who they see as strong.

WHEN EIGHTS ARE STRESSED

For Eights, lust is their compulsion or passion. In Enneagram work, *lust* means something different—and much broader—than sexual lust. As Don Riso and Russ Hudson have suggested, lust can be experienced and expressed in many ways. "Eights," they say, "are 'lusty' in that they are driven by a constant need for intensity, control, and self-extension. Lust causes Eights to try to push everything in their lives—to assert themselves willfully." Lust leads them to insist on their own agenda, dominate group dynamics, and stand their ground rather than seeking compromise. The result of all of that is trouble, and that trouble is what causes stress.

Eights almost always have their guard up. They're courageous, they take on battles for those they love, and they argue fiercely for justice. But in order to do all of that, they must repress their own tenderness and vulnerability. That is costly because showing a willingness to be vulnerable is the foundation for connecting with other people. And most of the stress in the life of an Eight includes problems with communication and struggles in relationship with others.

It is very stressful for Eights when they aren't in control because being controlled means they haven't been able to protect themselves from being betrayed or used by others for their agendas. When they're not in control, they have to move from managing situations and scenarios (which inadvertently includes managing other people) to partnership, which is usually only of interest to Eights when they are partnering up the ladder and not down.

Richard Rohr has said many times and in many settings that suffering is "whenever you are not in control." That is certainly true for Enneagram Eights. More than any other number, it's hard for them to accept that control is an illusion. Being strong and powerful is important to them along with achieving their objectives, but in excess it can be self-defeating. And their Enneagram compulsion to lust is by definition prone to excess. When Eights experience a loss of control, they often initially respond with behavior that doesn't serve them well. With every sense of diminishing power and control, the intensity of their feelings increases as does their combativeness and arrogance.

One of the most uncomfortable feelings for Eights is being betwixt and between, or in the unpredictability and uncertainty of liminal space. They are historically on the move, making things happen and shaping the future. In times when Eights can't take charge or

Eights almost always have their guard up.

when their ability to influence the behavior of other people or the outcome of things that are happening around them is limited, it leads to stress. Keep in mind that what is stressful for most numbers—a fiery argument, a tight deadline, an argument at work, a crucial decision—is home base for Eights. So, it takes a lot for them to experience the kind of feelings the rest of us have much more often. The pandemic of 2020, however, was the perfect trigger for Eights' anger and stress over their lack of ability to control just about anything.

THE MOVE TO FIVE IN STRESS

When stressed we all exaggerate our normal behavior. For Eights that suggests they will be bad tempered in a way that affects everyone. They are always concerned about being betrayed. When they're in stress, they make up scenarios where those around them are being disloyal or dishonest, which is usually not the case. An example would be an Eight deciding that someone or a group is an enemy and attacking them before they are attacked or betrayed.

Following stress and bad behavior when they are unhealthy in their number, Eights move to Five, but it's not straightforward. They could move to the high, healthy side of Five or they could settle for a lateral move from one unhealthy place to another. When they move to the low side of Five, where they slow down and stop doing, Eights find their usually high level of energy accumulates to the point it may disrupt their sleep or other patterns of behavior. Eights at their best struggle to be in touch with their feelings (because of their focus on doing), and in unhealthy Five space that is exacerbated. They withdraw from others and may stay isolated unless something changes within them or in their environment. But there is another option.

With Enneagram wisdom and some work, Eights can learn to intentionally seek behavior that defines healthy Fives. In that chosen move, they can use thinking to step back and see people and situations from a different perspective. One of the common reasons Eights experience stress is that they are overcommitted and overtired. In healthy Five space, they retreat, take time, and reorganize their commitments. They slow down and think things through before making decisions. They try to understand things from the perspective of both a participant (Eight) and an observer (Five). Having achieved a different way of seeing things, they can then reengage with a broader understanding of themselves and others, with less need for control.

THE KEY: MORE THINKING, LESS ANGER

For Eights who want to change their habitual behavior and make room for transformative experiences, the key to managing doing, their dominant center, begins with accepting the fact that they overexpress anger and underexpress other feelings. They also need to recognize that their focus on doing means the three Centers of Intelligence are out of balance. They tend to get crosswise with other numbers because they pay too little attention to thinking and feeling in their drive to do. And that may diminish the effectiveness of their doing. While we might think that paying attention to feeling is the key (because of the role of anger in their lives), Eights also need to engage more with thinking,

> Eights seem to have unending amounts of confidence, but along with the rest of us they struggle with insecurity.

especially thinking about the consequences of their actions. We might say that Eights "shoot first and aim second." If someone questions their actions, they think fast enough to explain why they did what they did, after the fact. But there is still unnecessary fallout because they reacted instead of choosing to think first. All that constant doing is not worth the disconnects and potential destructiveness that can result without enough consideration of their behavior. The same is true for feeling. If they are aware and intentional, Eights can recognize the feelings as they arise. They can stop and name what they're feeling, then think through what they're about to do. And then respond.

TRY THIS

PRACTICES FOR EIGHTS IN MANAGING DOING

- Be aware when you are behaving predictably and habitually. It can be soothing, but it is nonproductive.
- Practice vulnerability by participating in groups where you aren't the leader, and allow softer feelings without converting them into anger.

■ Allow people to take care of you sometimes.

■ Learn to delay expressions of your own feelings—especially anger. (You do this when you engage with the healthy side of Five.) Anger is all too easy for you to access, and remember that it protects you from your more tender and vulnerable feelings.

■ Be aware of when you are ignoring the importance of feelings: yours and others. Relationships should be considered in your journey toward doing what is yours to do.

■ Practice stepping back from assigning blame. Because your way of knowing comes from the deepest part of your being, you will always struggle to be flexible once you've made up your mind.

■ Recognize how hard it is for you to admit when you're wrong.

■ Be aware that while for you intensity is intimacy, that isn't true for every number.

■ Explore whether people move away from you or toward you. Consider what it feels like when you notice people backing away from you.

■ Be wary of dualistic thinking. Holistic, both/and thinking is almost always better than an either-or way of seeing the world. Most disagreements between people or groups are a compilation of mistakes and mistaken ideas from both sides.

■ Learn to delegate. It will serve you if you master it well.

■ Notice when you feel bored. It's probably masking other emotions.

■ Understand that others' small oversights are not a betrayal of trust.

■ Notice that a feeling of sadness is often an indicator of other honest feelings.

■ When compromise becomes necessary, be sure you own your part. Be mindful of your desire for all or nothing—either control or withdrawal.

■ Be aware that you are the most misunderstood number on the Enneagram; your passion is often misunderstood. Learn to allow yourself to acknowledge hurt and grieve losses and misunderstandings.

THE MOVE TO TWO IN SECURITY

There is a significant difference between security and confidence. Eights seem to have unending amounts of confidence, but along with the rest of us they struggle with insecurity. When Eights are in a healthy, secure place, they have access to some of the behavior and wisdom of a Two. When they feel safe in their relationships, they are more comfortable and more enjoyable. It's risky for them to choose vulnerability, yet it's a requirement for accessing a Two's way of being in the world. Eights can be tender and compassionate human beings. Unfortunately, sometimes others don't see or experience either one because Eights can be too busy, too bold, and too bossy out of habit. When they're in a healthy space, Eights filter decisions through their hearts as well as their minds and are more likely to sense the needs of others and help meet them.

One of the mysteries about Eights lies in the fact that they have absolutely no awareness of their impact on other people. I suspect it's because they've spent their lives protecting themselves from the influence of others. It's for that reason that I insist they are the most misunderstood number on the Enneagram. When they discover how they have hurt other people, it's usually a surprise, and it leaves them feeling shocked and confused and sad because they are limited in their understanding of all the ways people are hurt. It's a mindset that suggests, "If I didn't intend to hurt you, then why are you taking it personally? It isn't personal." But with some Two energy, the Eight capacity to sense others' needs and feelings increases.

Eights don't hurt other people intentionally. They are usually just focused on doing. Be assured, when Eights are healthy and integrated, they are more willing to let others lead or make suggestions. They learn to use their power for nurturing others and relate to most people as equals. They are compassionate and willing to sacrifice themselves for the sake of other people. Then others know they have been loved from a deep and honest place. And because Eights are always looking for a place they can trust, they are concerned with creating a trusting space for others.

9s

DECIDE MORE, MERGE LESS

My friend Brett told me about the time he and his wife and kids went to visit his dad, who lives out in the country off a gravel road. As he recalled: "A bumpy cattle guard lies across the gate at the entrance to my dad's house. As we left their house for our long drive back home, my wife decided she'd start out driving. She brought a travel mug filled to the very brim with hot coffee but with no lid. She set it in the cupholder and began to drive away.

"As we approached the cattleguard, my eyes darted from her to the cup, back to her, back to the cup. When we drove over the cattle guard, all of Newton's laws were realized at once—coffee sloshing all over the front seats of our car. Having identified the problem, I realized quickly I actually could have done something about it: you know, pick up the mug so it wouldn't slosh. But this epitomized my doing-dominant and doing-repressed nature—identifying a problem but not thinking I had anything to do with the solution."

THE NINE WAY OF SEEING THE WORLD

Nines have the least energy of all the numbers on the Enneagram because they are managing both internal and external boundaries. They want to keep out anything that would steal their peace and keep in anything that might cause trouble. To preserve energy, Nines are somewhat preoccupied with containment of both physical energy and anger. They believe if they can avoid the anger within themselves, they are less likely to find themselves in conflict with other people. Nines merge. They go along with others' agendas because they don't think they should assert themselves. They don't see themselves as important, and they're afraid of fragmentation in relationships.

Here are some other things to keep in mind about Nines:

- Nines sometimes don't know what they want and sometimes just aren't interested enough to invest the time and energy to find out. Or they may have a secret or private agenda but won't risk sharing it, fearing potential conflict. Nines often keep their thoughts to themselves.

- The Enneagram Nine's passion or sin is sloth, which has little to do with action or inaction and more to do with their desire to be unaffected by life, especially conflict.

- Nines are easygoing and pleasant to be with. I find them to be the least controlling of all personality types, and they seldom waste time and energy thinking about the behavior of other people.

- Healthy Nines serve as peacemakers and mediators throughout their lives. They're able to agree with possibilities and ideas from several points of view, without fully committing to any of them. They can easily identify with the ideas, philosophies, and beliefs of other people without needing to share their own.

- When others are reacting, Nines are usually centered and calm. They're receptive, optimistic, and peaceful.

- Nines may obsess over a decision, but that doesn't mean they're in a hurry to make it. And they're quite capable of being stubborn about choosing. But once they make a decision, they can be equally stubborn about holding to their choice.

WHEN NINES ARE STRESSED

When the world starts to get to Nines and they can't be as accommodating as usual, the stress leads them to disengage. They ignore their own desires and ambitions. They seem less grounded, and they begin to disconnect from the people they live and work with. It's subtle, but others feel it. Nines who are in more average than healthy space struggle to maintain their own tranquility, and they become more reactive to others' behavior.

> Nines have the least energy of all the numbers on the Enneagram because they are managing both internal and external boundaries.

For example, when a Nine is moving from average to unhealthy space, they become intolerant of other drivers. My Joe will say things like, "How did they pass the driving test?" or "Did you see that woman cross four lanes to make a right-hand turn? Unbelievable!"

I meet very few people who know Nines who don't agree heartily any time I tell this little story. Think about it. When they give in to this bad behavior, Nines are alone or with people they know well while driving. The terrible, inept drivers who are sharing the road have no idea they are being critiqued and disparaged with such severity, so Nines give themselves permission to be angry. And unless excessive honking and gestures are exchanged, negative consequences are unlikely. When a Nine does this sort of thing, you can tell that all is not well somewhere in the Nine's life. They might not be able to name what's wrong immediately, but in time they will know. In less secure situations when Nines are behaving badly, they are using most of their available energy to suppress their anger.

They are often even more stubborn than usual, particularly when it comes to sharing what's wrong.

Nines who are overwhelmed resort to numbing themselves, sometimes in obvious ways such as with drugs or alcohol but also by too much sleeping, eating, shopping, playing video games, or watching television. Some waste time playing more than enough golf, riding horses, participating in sports leagues, or more subdued activities like reading, crafting, or sewing. The activity is not nearly as important as their desire to be unaffected by what's happening in their lives, which is the true definition of sloth.

THE MOVE TO SIX IN STRESS

In stress, when they are aware of conflict that may or may not involve them or are feeling distressed at something they failed to do, Nines move to Six. If they move to the unhealthy side of Six, they may temporarily lose the optimism and faith that sustains them most of the time. They may waste energy, which is limited, by planning for the worst thing that could happen even though it's unlikely. And they will begin to pull back from what they say is "just too much" of what is stressing them.

Using Enneagram wisdom, Nines can learn to choose the best of Six. For example, it can be good for Nines to be exposed to some of the anxiety and worry of Six because sometimes Nines are so laid back they aren't concerned enough. Nines tend to subscribe to the belief that things will handle themselves. While that's sometimes true, often it is not. And some anxiety has the potential to push Nines into action. One of the best possibilities on the Enneagram comes when Nines find their voice by accessing some good Six energy. They are more willing to speak out on their own behalf and they're more intentional about the important things. They decide more and merge less and give extra energy to the relationships that matter. Instead of procrastinating, they invest in new ways to work on projects that may have been pushed aside for another time.

Nines have the most unique place on the Enneagram. From their place at the top, they often know more about the desires of the cascading numbers around the circle than they do about their own. They sometimes merge with image and conformity in Three, and at other times with the Six fondness for authority and rules. Nines are caught between wanting approval and wanting to disobey, and they solve the problem by not choosing either one.

THE KEY: CLAIM YOUR PART

As one of the three core numbers on the Enneagram, Nines are both doing dominant and doing repressed. That means they use their senses to take in information from the world, assessing what should be done. But then they don't use the Doing Center to process or make sense of the information they've received—or to act. For example, a Nine might walk into a room and notice something that needs attention but then think, "Someone should get in here and do something about all of this." So the key for Nines in managing doing is to ask in real time, "Is this my responsibility?" If the answer is yes, then they need to ask, "How do I respond?" In order for Nines to take action at the appropriate time, they have to be willing to assert themselves, allow themselves to act, and know that their participation matters.

TRY THIS

PRACTICES FOR NINES IN MANAGING DOING
- Be aware when you are withholding your personal opinions or desires. Recognize that you have something worthwhile to contribute.

- Learn to use deadlines and the structuring of steps for completing projects as a way to stay focused on your responsibilities.

- Focus on the next right thing that needs to be done rather than on the whole project or goal. Don't let the magnitude of the whole prevent you from taking specific steps toward achieving specific tasks.

- Take a stand. Make a decision. You can always change your mind later.

- Since it is easier for you to know what you don't want than to know what you do, ask for choices. Then choose one.

- Engage in conversations and stay engaged from beginning to end. Avoid dipping in and out when you sense potential conflict or discomfort.

- When you are gathering information, be sure to take the next step to plan what you will do with it. Then do it.

- Be aware when you are behaving predictably and habitually. It can be soothing, but it is often nonproductive.

- When you feel you are being pushed, be aware of your responses. Are you growing more and more stubborn? Is it necessary?

- Last, but certainly not least, remember: "later" is not a point in time.

THE MOVE TO THREE IN SECURITY

There's no doubt that the Nines' tendency to choose, habitually or intentionally, to be unaffected by life and their environment can be problematic. But there are also times when it can be helpful. Their way of seeing makes it possible for them to establish a place of peace and harmony within themselves. And when they're healthy they often try to create a peaceful environment around and beyond themselves for those they care about.

Healthy Nines have some access to the behavior and gifts of a Three. They are distinctly separate individuals who know what they want. When the best of Nine and Three is combined, Nines are self-confident. They are more committed to discovering and developing their own gifts and talents. In this space Nines don't live through others, they live with them, acting on their environment in a good way. One of their best qualities stands out when they're not intimidated because they can assert themselves without being aggressive. And the world certainly needs more of that.

It's a joy to encounter Nines when they are secure and well-integrated. They aren't struggling with inertia; they take more control of their own lives, and they know their own value. Along with all of the numbers on the Enneagram, Nines have a lot to offer the rest of us when we're living through some kind of liminality and when times are complicated. Living with mystery isn't easy. And it's particularly hard for those of us who live in the West. We're accustomed to answers and some control over our lives. The calming, assuring presence of a Nine can mitigate some of the negative effects of such strange times. They are patient and exude a sense of peace they make available to all of us.

1s

TWO THINGS CAN BE TRUE

Noah, our second oldest grandson, might be a One on the Enneagram. Joe and I were excited to have second-row seats for his graduation from kindergarten. Five- and six-year-old boys are often not too concerned about whether or not their shirts are tucked in, and hair is sometimes more of an expression than a style. But for Noah those things have always been important. He memorizes all of the rules for any environment he finds himself in, I suspect because he's hoping to be noticed for being a good boy, which of course he is.

At the ceremony, the kindergarten class took the stage, always somehow cuter than the grades that went before or will come after them. Like most kindergarten graduations, this one included the little ones singing songs that had to do with potential and possibility. Noah stood tall in the first row, singing his heart out and having a really great time until he forgot the rules his teacher had given him and put his hand in his pocket. The sadness I saw come over his face was heartbreaking. Some among our four children and nine grandchildren wouldn't care at all. But Noah is one who does.

THE ONE WAY OF SEEING THE WORLD

Ones are dogged by an ever-present inner critic: a relentless inner voice that points out every time they make a mistake, are late, wrong, unprepared, overdressed, underdressed, unsuccessful, too successful, talking too much or too little. Control is of utmost importance to Ones, but it's focused on their own belief that they have the correct definition of what's right and wrong. Like Eights, the first person they want to control is themselves, but their lack of healthy boundaries leads to their attempts to control other people too. They may succeed, but others often resent it because of the Ones' self-righteous, critical approach.

Here are some other things to keep in mind about Ones:

- It's important to Ones to measure up and to be respected. Unfortunately, the only way they can measure their standing is by comparing themselves to others, which inevitably leads to competition. All competition leads to winners and losers, and it's very hard for Ones when they lose.

- Standards of behavior are really important to Ones because from their perspective there is only one right way to do things. Ones talk about how we *should* act, what we *should* feel, who we *should* be, and what we *should* do. Sometimes those mandates are so overemphasized they leave little room for feelings and relationships and objectivity.

- In Ones, their compulsion to anger takes the form of resentment. As Don Riso and Russ Hudson say, "Anger in itself is not the problem; in Ones the anger is repressed, leading to continued frustration and dissatisfaction with themselves and the world."

- Ones turn feelings of anger in on themselves first and then they try to manage their guilt or shame by finding fault with and blaming others. One of my favorite sayings, which I learned from the recovery community, is that all expectations are resentments waiting to happen. For Ones, it's the expectations they have for themselves that create the greatest burden.

WHEN ONES ARE STRESSED

Ones in average to unhealthy space are trapped in a pattern of trying to control their natural drives and desires. They are drawn to ideal behavior, and it takes a lot of good spiritual direction and personal work for them to learn to be patient with themselves, to give themselves mercy and grace. In the absence of that opportunity, Ones fall into the trap of striving for perfection, which makes it hard for them to accept anything as it is. And since there is imperfection everywhere, stress is inevitable.

> Be good to yourself. You are worthy of pleasure and all the goodness that comes your way.

When stressed, Ones, like all types, exaggerate their normal behavior. That means doubling down on insisting that everything be done correctly, according to an ever-rising benchmark that magically separates good enough from perfect. How can a person live up to that day after day? The answer, according to Ones, is discipline. Ones I know have taught me that they structure their lives in a way that sustains their values. That sounds good, but it is fraught with problems. Because when Ones adopt a value for their lives, it's forever. Changing their minds would be an admission that they were mistaken—that is, imperfect—and that won't do at all.

The heartfelt desire that Ones have to do things correctly, and to be right and good in what they do and how they do it, is admirable. I am humbled by how hard they work to do the right thing, the right way, regardless of personal cost. But the truth is moderation in all things is a reasonable and responsible way for all of us to live life.

When a One walks into a room, they see everything that is wrong. Keep in mind that we can never change how we see—we can only change what we do with how we see. To that end, Ones try to be fair-minded and honest. They notice everything and they work diligently to avoid expressing anger directly. And at the same time, they are easily frustrated when others don't have the same ability or even desire to recognize and correct their own faults without prompting. Ones have absolute standards; it is a struggle for them to understand that whether or not something can be labeled a fault is in the eye of the beholder. The less people around them seem to care about doing things right, the more that seems wrong to Ones, which makes them more stressed and more committed to the notion that there is a right and wrong way to behave.

In stress, Ones can become intolerant and self-righteous, and are often obsessed with the perception of corruption they find in others while ignoring their own contradictory actions. They get angry when other people don't try as hard as they do, and in their frustration and dissatisfaction they begin to perfect what they can. It might be the yard, the garage, wearing (or not wearing) a mask during a pandemic, or the way clothes are arranged in a closet. This response of doing to manage the rising anger is an intuitive tool to avoid resorting to rage.

In my love for Ones, it's helpful for me to remember that unless they can find fault in other people, there is no way for them to level the playing field enough to even find a place to stand.

THE MOVE TO FOUR IN STRESS

Ones in stress follow the arrow on the Enneagram diagram from their number to Four. I've learned that the first sign of moving to the unhealthy side of Four is beginning to long for an idealized person or situation to complete their life. They pull inward, where the critic lives, and begin to feel melancholy. Sometimes that is followed by depression, but not always. And in Four space, they focus inward instead of outward, which is more normal for them.

The inner focus reduces the amount they are able to accomplish, which makes them feel worse.

Unhealthy One combined with the low side of Four is the place where Ones become hopeless, cynical, and sarcastic. They become more rigid, and in a strange way they find their anger comforting. But the comfort is replaced with shame when they realize what it can cost them and the people they love.

With some of the behavior and wisdom of healthy Four, Ones touch deep, new places that fill their souls in ways that perceived perfection cannot. They are more creative and less critical. Father Richard Rohr, who is a One, points out that for Ones, either everything belongs, or nothing belongs. In healthy Four space, Ones are drawn to holistic thinking. They can entertain both/and thinking and have greater appreciation for out-of-the box thinking. Ones also find that they have access to feelings that don't need fixing. And the best news of all is that the critic cannot be as loud about feelings as it is about actions.

> Happiness is a legitimate response to life.

Ones have discipline that most of us lack. They are still deeply committed to doing the right thing. They're willing to make more sacrifices than most to achieve the goals they set for themselves. And they can find part of what they need for the journey on the healthy side of Four.

THE KEY: CONTROL YOUR INNER CRITIC

Ones are those among us who grew up aware of and following the rules. Safety included being responsible, behaving properly, and above all being seen as "good" in the eyes of the authority figures in their lives. Ones are very hard on themselves because of their focus on perfection, which takes the form of doing to try to achieve. As they learn to assert more and more control over the inner critic, they will be slower in automatically responding by doing. Instead they can learn to use that energy for more productive thinking. When they feel anger rising in their bodies, it's difficult to know if they are angry with themselves or their inner critic or others, so they convert anger into action as a means of control. The only time they can avoid this limitation is when they are sure of their correctness, which is infrequent and never lasts long. If they can claim their anger rather than referring to it as another emotion like weariness or frustration, they can avoid the inclination to manage it with doing. When Ones are sure of their correctness, they have a lot of energy, but they need to learn to be careful to use it productively —and not just in the pursuit of more perfection.

TRY THIS

PRACTICES FOR ONES IN MANAGING DOING

- Don't listen to the voice of the inner critic. The inner critic is *not* your friend!
- Put boundaries around the idea of perfection and embrace the idea that, while many things are not perfect, they are good enough. Accept that it's possible to feel secure even when surrounded by imperfection.
- Ask yourself if there really is only one right way to do things. Seeing only one right way to do things prevents compromise and collaboration, and it damages relationships.
- Be aware of anger as it begins to rise in you. Call it by its name and see it for what it is.
- Be aware that compulsive doing can be an intuitive release of anger, but compulsive doing when used to avoid real priorities will not help you.

- Learn to pause when you feel anger rising until you feel something either in yourself or in your environment shift. That will help protect you and others from your anger.

- Focus more on what you really want and less on what you think should be done.

- Learn to ask for your needs to be met, rather than assuming that others will know what they are. Then graciously receive the gifts that come.

- Recognize that procrastination in the search for perfection is a problem. You need to tackle things you can't do perfectly and just do your best.

- Create a ritual or a practice you can return to again and again that will remind you that perceived perfection does not assure security.

- Work toward having messy fun at least once a week.

- Be good to yourself. If you don't work on anything listed here, work on this one! You are worthy of pleasure and all the goodness that comes your way. Embrace it and then pass it on.

THE MOVE TO SEVEN IN SECURITY

Healthy Ones have the ability to relate impartially to the environment. They have some balance that allows them to act with wisdom and conviction. They are conscientious, but they aren't burdened with the belief that what seems right for them is right for everyone. They're socially charming, and they can support the agendas, hopes, and dreams of others without any effort to control the outcome. Unfortunately, even in healthy space, they offer more grace to others than they can manage for themselves.

When Ones are in a healthy and secure place, they have access to some of the behavior and wisdom of Seven. This is one of my favorite moves on the Enneagram. When healthy Ones move toward Seven, they experience a freedom that they struggle to describe. My dad, a One, used to say, "Everything begins to change when I know I'm headed for the cabin in Colorado with the time to fish until I get my fill. I get excited long before we get in the car!" Most Ones tell me that their favorite memories were created when they were away from home and unburdened by responsibilities. They tell stories about little indiscretions and they laugh about unexpected fun that was part of a well-planned but unpredictable trip. Happiness is a legitimate response to life. With a little influence from Seven, Ones can give in to feeling happiness long enough for those feelings to turn into joy.

Integrated Ones don't think they have to make everything perfect, and they are able to move from obligation to enthusiasm and from restraint to freedom. They understand serenity as being able to hold two opposing views at the same time without having to choose one over the other. They are flexible without compromising their values, and they are full of natural gifts that they offer freely to an imperfect world. To every One who reads this sentence, please know that you are good, all the way through and beyond.

Part Two

STANCES

NAMING AND MANAGING YOUR REPRESSED CENTER OF INTELLIGENCE

THE SOUL WORK OF THE REPRESSED CENTER

have always been someone who went to church. I grew up in the United Methodist Church, which is now my spiritual home, but I also spent some years as a Roman Catholic, more as a result of circumstances than anything else. Going to church, I discovered, is not the same as doing the work of spiritual formation. I tried to begin that work in my early thirties, but unfortunately my commitment didn't match my desired outcome. I see now that I wasn't mature enough to make it a priority, except during times when my world seemed to be falling apart and my answers to the problems I faced seemed wholly inadequate.

By the time I turned thirty-five, I had new reasons to want to grow spiritually, and by thirty-seven I was committed to a regular daily practice. Looking back now, I know it was all part of the rhythm of life that necessarily includes change. Some change we choose and some change we allow, and some change is nonnegotiable. Not to choose at all is death in one way or another.

I have come to believe that it's important to live an intentional life. But it's really hard. It requires awareness, which is exhausting, and it requires discipline and faith and compassion. And I've found it's worth it because it frees my soul and then I can take steps toward personal and spiritual transformation. It was a big surprise to me to find out that my soul is my business too. Until then, I believed my soul was complete and that I might do something that could *hurt* it, but I didn't know I could *grow* it.

Kathleen Hurley and Theodorre Donson are unsung heroes of the Enneagram, and it was some of their work that introduced me to the concept of growing my soul. They suggested that if our souls are going to grow, each of us needs to accept the responsibility for developing them. Most of us have never been told that we needed to do this kind of work.

So then what they said next really stuck with me: "An underdeveloped soul cannot protect us from automatically reacting to the cares and anxieties of life." Think about it: our Enneagram numbers are all about the ways we *react*—habitually and automatically—to life, one episode at a time. And there is no coherence, no sense of integration, of those episodes. In fact, for some people, all of their energy is wrapped up in these episodes, so if there is no episode, they create one. Hurley and Donson call it "the world of constant cares." Regardless of what you call it, there are people who are living their lives without learning from their experiences. Their souls are wedded to the world of constant cares, and they don't have the necessary tools or practices to make better and different choices.

Mary Oliver named for us the reality that we have this "one wild and precious life." I think we all want to live life to the fullest, but we're not sure how.

Years of studying the wisdom of the Enneagram have led me to an ever-deepening understanding of how we are broken and how we can be healed, often at exactly the same time. The Enneagram reveals who you are and who you can become. If you don't know yourself, how will you ever know who you are in relation to others and who you are in relation to God? It seems that maybe we have spent far too much time growing our personalities and not nearly enough time growing our souls.

But the Enneagram is not a solution. It's a tool for engaging in a nonstatic process. And it's better if you combine it with other spiritual practices that increase your soul awareness and help you begin to live from the fullness of all that you are instead of merely your personality. Your personality is fantastic, but it's thin. There is so much more to who you are and who you can become than your personality alone.

The Enneagram serves as a bridge over what I believe are the first two hurdles for most people who begin a spiritual journey toward transformation. We encounter the first hurdle when we begin to move toward a new awareness of who we are and who we can be, but we run into all of the things we don't like about ourselves. They seem impossible to change. Then, if we can embrace that challenge, the second hurdle we're faced with is the pain we all bring from growing up in our families of origin, where we hurt one another whether we intended to or not.

The Enneagram is so helpful with both! In learning our numbers, we can finally understand ourselves and why we do the things we do. At the same time, it teaches us about the people we call family, who represent some of the other eight personality types, making a way for us to offer the same grace to others that we desire for ourselves.

STANCES AND BALANCE

The purpose of the first section of this book was to identify the Enneagram triad you belong to based on your dominant Center of Intelligence. Then, using the movements with and against the arrows on the Enneagram, we looked at its wisdom when it comes to managing stress and security. We saw that if we are to manage stress in our lives, then we will have to manage our dominant Center of Intelligence.

The next important step is to continue the process of learning to balance thinking, feeling, and doing. To understand how to achieve that balance, we need to know and understand the concept of stances. While triads are determined by which of the centers we prefer, stances are determined by the center that we learned to protect (and thus repress) because our use of it was misunderstood during childhood.

The stances indicate how each type tries to get its primary needs met, and they are divided according to which center is repressed. By repressed, I don't mean that the center is unused or weak, just that it is underused in comparison to the other two centers. That's why people who have repressed thinking can have multiple degrees but not think productively. People who repress feeling can have lots of successful relationships but not know what they themselves truly feel. And people who repress doing can responsibly manage their jobs with great efficiency but may not always do the right thing.

The lack of balance means that the three centers are often not used for their intended purpose. Thinking is for gathering information and then sorting it into its proper place in our brains. We need to use it for planning and for analyzing people and situations. Feeling is acknowledging other people's needs and agendas. And of course, it's necessary in building and maintaining relationships. Doing is for accomplishing. It is the energy behind pleasure seeking and taking care of ourselves.

THE LOSS OF BALANCE

Imbalance is learned early in life. During childhood, when we protect and repress one of our centers rather than risk using it, we use it less and less as we grow. Here's what this might look like. When my parents adopted me, they already had two biological sons who were fifteen and eighteen years old, and that was the general age range of my cousins and the children of my parents' friends. As a little one, I learned quickly that no one really cared what I was thinking about. If I offered a contribution to the conversation, the adults were loving but patronizing. But when I learned to read their feelings and then respond to them, they thought I was "adorable" or "precious" or even at times "precocious." So I stopped using thinking to make my way and capitalized on my ability to interpret and respond to others' feelings.

> I have come to believe that it's important to live an intentional life. But it's really hard.

There are many children whose parents or other authority figures frequently responded to their tears or sadness by telling them that they don't have any reason to cry and that they should stop immediately. Many, if not most, of those children learned that it is not helpful to allow—much less share—feelings, so they began to rely on thinking and doing because it resulted in approval and therefore safety.

Many children often choose tasks that are just beyond their reach, like helping bake a birthday cake. But trying out the electric mixer in order to be helpful turns into regret and tears because there is a mess to be cleaned up (and quite possibly accompanied by a lecture that begins with "Why would you do *that*?"). After a number of similar experiences with trying to do something, these children resort to feeling and thinking in their effort to receive compliments and comfort.

People around us have expectations that we will behave in a certain way, and most children catch on to those expectations (implicit and explicit) at a very early age. So the process of imbalance develops in two ways: first in how children interpret information through their senses, and then in how they process, or make sense of, that information.

The dynamics among the three centers means that

- the preferred or *dominant* center moves forward to interpret information that is received through the senses. Its values dominate the way information is processed (for me, this was feeling).

- the *support* center joins the dominant center in processing that information (in my case, doing).

- the *repressed* center is dormant and protected (for me, that was thinking).

In this dynamic, two Centers of Intelligence are doing the work of three, so they are overworked and tired. Only a few of their values are being used. The confusion that follows often means agendas are tangled up and the wrong center gets involved in responding to situations.

THE DEPENDENT, WITHDRAWING, AND AGGRESSIVE STANCES

How we take in information and process it is very important because the way we make sense of things creates our worldview or our particular philosophy of life, and our worldview is the basis for our actions. It was shocking to me as a Two when I learned from Enneagram wisdom that for the most part, I only use two of the three centers (feeling and doing) in how I understand the world.

> We have spent far too much time growing our personalities and not nearly enough time growing our souls.

Every number has a similar pattern. The three Centers of Intelligence are our natural resources. We all have all three, but we don't use them all!

Depending on the dynamics among our three Centers of Intelligence and our type's worldview, we tend to take a particular stance, that is, a way of being. Enneagram teaching about this concept is drawn partly from the work of psychologist Karen Horney, who said that there are three responses to encounters with others: we either move *away* from other people, *toward* other people, or *against* other people. Enneagram teachers Maria Beesing, Robert Nogosek, and Patrick O'Leary took that further and divided Enneagram personalities according to three categories:

Dependent types: those who move toward others

Aggressive types: those who move against or, as I now say, stand independent of others

Withdrawing types: those who move away from others

Those are the terms we will use in the following chapters. The work of stances is to understand how that dynamic plays out for each number and to see how you can access the potential and gifts of the repressed center. This is how we begin to foster balance among all three Centers of Intelligence.

THE ENNEAGRAM CENTERS OF INTELLIGENCE AND STANCES

NUMBER	TRIAD	STANCE	PREFERRED AND DOMINANT CENTER	SUPPORT CENTER	REPRESSED CENTER
One	Gut	Dependent	Doing	Feeling	Thinking
Two	Heart	Dependent	Feeling	Doing	Thinking
Three	Heart	Aggressive	Feeling	Thinking / Doing* Doing / Thinking	Feeling
Four	Heart	Withdrawing	Feeling	Thinking	Doing
Five	Head	Withdrawing	Thinking	Feeling	Doing
Six	Head	Dependent	Thinking	Feeling / Doing Doing / Feeling	Thinking
Seven	Head	Aggressive	Thinking	Doing	Feeling
Eight	Gut	Aggressive	Doing	Thinking	Feeling
Nine	Gut	Withdrawing	Doing	Thinking / Feeling Feeling / Thinking	Doing

*The core numbers Three, Six, and Nine are both dominant and repressed in the same Center of Intelligence. In the support center, one will lead, the other will follow.

Please be aware that developing the repressed center becomes the great challenge of Enneagram work. And it is work you will need to do for the rest of your life. But it's worth it. It is transformational and creates spiritual vitality, and it truly makes all the difference.

CHAPTER FOUR

THE WITHDRAWING STANCE

MOVING AWAY FROM OTHERS

At a recent get-together with my family and a few close friends, I observed that several of them were in the Withdrawing Stance: our youngest son, BJ, is a Four; our close friend John is a Five; and my husband, Joe, daughter Jenny, and son-in-law Billy are all Nines. Even though they share the same stance, when we were all together, I saw how it manifested itself differently for each of them depending on their number.

BJ is an extrovert who, like other Fours I know, sometimes struggles to present himself in ways that he believes will be acceptable and desirable—even to those of us who love him most. As a Four, BJ understands that doing is highly valued in our culture and in our family, which meant that he brought what we asked him to, plus something else. Then in order to feel good about his contribution, he asked several of us if we liked it or if it was prepared the right way. BJ, like most Fours, was trying to do something special as a way of making a place for himself that was worthy of attention but that wouldn't expose any feelings of inadequacy and vulnerability. I am always aware that our social gatherings are tricky for BJ; he doesn't know quite what to do, so he sometimes says or does more than he needs to.

When John, Joe's horseback-riding buddy who is a prominent pulmonologist and dear friend, joined the party, he was on call from the hospital. This meant that he came in and out of conversations with us. We knew that he wanted to be included, and I was aware that engaging with both worlds is costly, both in time and energy for him as a Five. He was processing and keeping straight all of the information he was carrying in his head, both personal and professional, while trying to be present to us. We gave him some space to settle in, allowing for the difference in the amount of time we wanted to spend with him and the amount of time and energy he had to give. Because whatever we get from John is always worth it.

My Nine son-in-law, Billy, was, as usual, both present and withdrawn at the same time. He was there in the house hanging out with us or outside playing with the kids, but I didn't hear his voice much. Later, when he was grilling the burgers and hot dogs, he sometimes got distracted, as Nines often do, and left the grill to take care of something else or investigate what the kids were into. That's typical doing dominant and doing repressed Nine behavior. Billy was almost always helping to do something to get our dinner on the table, but he wasn't always timely. Knowing the Enneagram like we do, we all laughed about the difference between regular time and "Nine time." As late afternoon approached, I was aware that Billy had moved to the edges, along with BJ and John. He was listening more than participating or talking, but he was still connected in ways that were obvious. He wasn't interested in gossip, nor did he need to make a point about anything he didn't agree with. He was willing to tell us what he thought if we asked, but he didn't need any of us to agree with him, and he wasn't disappointed if we didn't.

By the end of the day, BJ, John, and Billy were on the outside looking in. They had talked a little, listened a lot, participated in whatever games they were invited to join, enjoyed several one-on-one conversations, loved on the littles, and kept the peace. While the rest of us—a mix of just about all the Enneagram numbers—were busy with our own preoccupations, our three withdrawing numbers were, each in their own way, managing their energy and reflecting peace.

THE THREE REALITIES OF REPRESSED DOING

Fours, Fives, and Nines make up the Withdrawing Stance. By *withdrawing*, we mean that they repress doing—the ability to act and to affect their world—and look within themselves to survive. Their inner world is the real world for them. By leaving out doing, thinking and feeling are combined in supportive roles.

- For Fours, feeling is dominant. This means that thinking supports feeling, so Fours take in information using the Feeling Center, and then they make sense of it using feeling and thinking.

- For Fives, thinking is dominant and feeling supports thinking. This means that Fives take in information using the Thinking Center, and then they make sense of it using thinking and feeling.

- As one of the core numbers on the Enneagram, Nines are both doing dominant *and* doing repressed. That simply means that they take in information from the environment using their dominant center (doing), as defined by their triad. But they don't use doing to make sense of or decide what to do about the information they have received. As a result, either thinking or feeling will dominate the way Nines make sense of things. One will lead and the other will support.

THE WITHDRAWING STANCE

NUMBER	TRIAD	STANCE	PREFERRED AND DOMINANT CENTER	SUPPORT CENTER	REPRESSED CENTER
Four	Heart	Withdrawing	Feeling	Thinking	Doing
Five	Head	Withdrawing	Thinking	Feeling	Doing
Nine	Gut	Withdrawing	Doing	Thinking / Feeling Feeling / Thinking	Doing

Withdrawing as a descriptor for these numbers' stance means that because they repress the ability to act and to affect their world, they have to look within themselves to survive. Their inner world is the real world for them. They have told me that sometimes they feel sort of isolated, but that it doesn't bother them too much.

Fours use that feeling of isolation or lack of connection for fanciful thinking and imagining. And because of how they see, and how they incorporate what's happening into their ways of being a Four, their alone time, whether surrounded by people or actually by themselves, can be filled with color and texture and beauty.

> Withdrawing as a descriptor for these numbers' stance means that because they repress the ability to act and to affect their world, they have to look within themselves to survive.

For Fives, social connections are primarily for gathering information. They can view any perceived lack of connection as an opportunity to observe without the cost of lost energy.

Nines struggle because of how they see. They are always aware of at least two sides to everything and they are trying to keep in anything that would cause conflict while keeping out anything that would steal their peace. When feeling alone or isolated, Nines rest.

Fours, Fives, and Nines are all people who have an independent point of view. They get their strength from inside themselves and don't seek or need anyone else to agree with them or join them. And they don't react when others disagree with them or have a different point of view; they generally let others think and believe whatever they want. They're all observers, each number for its own reason.

Fours observe because they are accustomed to being misunderstood when they speak or act intuitively or too quickly.

Fives observe because, in response to their need to preserve energy, they learned to observe far more than participate.

And Nines observe because of their passion, which is sloth (defined in the Enneagram as their desire to be unaffected by life). Added to that, their preference for avoiding conflict makes observation before action a good way to prevent fragmentation in relationships.

All three numbers quietly count on their own strength to manage their lives. They easily change their focus from one thing to another depending on what grabs their attention. They don't shake things up and they seldom volunteer thoughts and ideas. In general, they simply don't make big statements or call attention to themselves in any overt way (the exception being Fours who have a big Three wing). I've learned from all three numbers that it's because they have so often felt misunderstood. For these reasons and more that we will discuss in the following chapters, their independence is the bedrock of their way of being in the

> **Unlike Aggressive and Dependent numbers who want other people to agree with them, those in the Withdrawing Stance are not influenced by what the crowd is saying or doing.**

world. Unlike Aggressive and Dependent numbers who want other people to agree with them, those in the Withdrawing Stance are not influenced by what the crowd is saying or doing.

It's important to remember that when people who make up the Withdrawing Stance enter a room, they are very self-conscious, and they tell me that they usually feel like they don't belong. They often say they feel like they don't have a "rightful place" in what's going on. And that they are unsure about how to participate in what's happening until they can figure it out. I see this all the time in our family gatherings, but since we all know the Enneagram, we have found ways of being comfortable together and even changing some of our behavior to support the Fours, Fives, and Nines while encouraging them to venture out into the world of doing.

On an ordinary day, when life is somewhat routine, all three numbers generally do what they want to do, which may not be what needs to be done. I'm not suggesting that they don't perform well at work, or that they are slackers regarding responsibilities in the groups they belong to. But I am suggesting that since they are doing repressed, they don't imagine that what needs to be done is theirs to do.

> **Each of the three numbers in the Withdrawing Stance is oriented to the past.**

They are missing the self-assurance, self-determination, and confidence that are learned by doing. In addition, they are often blind to the possibility that they should do something when other people are involved. They might analyze how something could be improved or even fixed. And they might suggest solutions or other ideas, but they rarely take the initiative to do something about it. They tell me that what *they* could do doesn't even cross their minds.

In his book *Consolations*, author and poet David Whyte suggests that maturity is the ability to "inhabit the past, the present, and the future all at once." In studying Enneagram stances, we know that each one is tethered primarily to past, present, or future. Whyte says, "Immaturity is shown by making false choices: living only in the past, or the present, or even, living in only two out of the three." It stands to reason, if Whyte is correct—and I believe he is—that we will have to recognize that we prefer one orientation to time and that we will need to find balance in that too if we are to achieve maturity as he explains it.

The Withdrawing Stance's Orientation to Time

Each of the three numbers in the Withdrawing Stance is oriented to the past. When focused on the past, Fours ruminate on relationships and conversations that are missing from their lives. Fives think about all of the information they have gathered, and then they use thinking to realign it into new systems. And Nines think about the way their lives were in both the distant and recent past. They consider the good and the bad, and they struggle with feeling powerless to improve what was good or repair what was bad. All three numbers think about people or conversations or what they've learned and how those fit with what they know. They are all ponderers. I understand pondering because I grew up around a lot of farmers and ranchers. They don't just think about things—they ponder, meaning they think long and carefully. And they allow extra time for really important decisions. For these numbers, time isn't for consulting other people like dependent types do. It is for pondering, which reduces the chance of making costly mistakes.

All three types handle difficult situations by being accommodating, but they silently resent it. They aren't practiced at standing up for themselves. When they finally decide to stand up for themselves it may be awkward or too forceful. We can all relate to that because it happens to all of us when we are inclined to act based on what we've learned from our stress number, or when we feel uncertain about how others will respond to us if we act on our own behalf.

Finally, all three withdrawing numbers have ideas and feelings and things they would like to do that they never follow through with because of the perceived cost. Many of those who make up this stance tell me that they daydream sometimes. And they have private thoughts, but I don't think they would call them secrets. It's nothing bad, there are just many things they don't share.

We all have our own way of managing stress as discussed in previous chapters. In addition to their stress moves (Fours moving to Two, Fives moving to Seven, and Nines moving to Six), all three numbers also tend to pull back and avoid confronting or addressing the source of their tension.

4s

CHOOSE THE ORDINARY

Fours see and interpret the world through feeling. They value relationships and interpersonal exchange. And along with every number in the Feeling Triad, image is very important for Fours, but they are not interested in stereotypical image as defined by cultural trends. They want to stand apart—or withdraw—from all of that while creating a style that they believe represents who they authentically are.

A Four's primary sense of meaning comes from relationships. Connecting with other people on a meaningful level is very fulfilling for them. They are inordinately emotionally sensitive at times, which is a reflection of how they see, but that can be a double-edged sword. At times, others find Fours too sensitive or find it challenging to believe their feelings are genuine. But of course there are times when others feel at home with the expressive nature of their personalities. Fours are usually happy to let their feelings show, but they are vigilant about making sure others appreciate them for who they are and what they are sharing.

Because Fours find their primary sense of meaning through relationships, perhaps the greatest challenge for Fours is that, because of a lack of self-confidence, they are often looking for someone who can complete them and with whom they can build a satisfying relationship. Of course, they know that successful relationships require mutuality, and they know they have a lot to offer. But at the same time, they believe that if they find the right person, that person will add what Fours are convinced is missing in themselves.

For Fours the support Center of Intelligence is thinking. So although they take in information with feeling, they make sense of it using both feeling and thinking. And in using those two centers, they are oriented to what's going on inside themselves and inside of others. In accessing these two centers, they are naturally analytical about feelings. They are very curious, and I think it's because they have both a vivid imagination and critical thinking skills.

> Self-assurance is often lacking in doing repressed numbers and that's a big problem because, unlike self-confidence, self-assurance includes trust in one's own character.

I have frequently asserted that Fours are the most complex number on the Enneagram, and they never question this. I think they know it to be true because they spend so much time and energy trying to understand why they are the way they are. Regrettably I taught for years that Fours want to be *special*. That was incorrect. So I changed and said that Fours want to be *unique*. But that was inadequate. The truth is, Fours want to be seen and heard and ultimately known and understood. And that takes time—the kind of time only a few are willing to give.

For Fours, doing is repressed, so they don't feel like they can affect their environment. That leaves them awash in feelings. Those feelings mandate that they take life in on a very personal level and then ruminate about it even when action is required. Fours do things, but frequently only the things they like or find life giving.

This means they have a tendency to ignore the practical parts of life, including mundane chores.

Fours struggle with hanging in there to finish things from projects to relationships. When things don't go well, they automatically assume that they are the problem. Their belief that they are inherently flawed in some way, coupled with their tendency to withdraw, leads them to think that if they just pull away the problem will be solved. That is seldom true and every Four needs to explore that because the shame that follows can be paralyzing. Self-assurance is often lacking in doing repressed numbers and that's a big problem because, unlike self-confidence, self-assurance includes trust in one's own character.

The Enneagram never leaves us without a solution, and the answer to our personality problems almost always begins with finding and learning to maintain balance. For the Withdrawing Stance the necessary balance can only be achieved by bringing up doing. In my experience, the Enneagram doesn't lend itself to pushing down the dominant center in an effort to balance all three. Instead, equilibrium is achieved by bringing up what is repressed.

KEYS FOR FOURS TO BRING UP DOING

If you are honest, you will find that your attention as a Four naturally goes to what is missing. You believe others have it, whatever "it" is, and you don't. From there you get trapped in "if only I could be____, then I would be____," and that path leaves you feeling ordinary at best and usually "less than." That focus on what's missing is expressed in your passion, which is envy, and that needs to be managed because you are otherwise trapped in wanting the comfort and peace that you believe is afforded to others but not you. If it was mere jealousy that you struggled with—if you wanted someone else's car, for example—then you could save your money or get a second job and buy the car. But to want another person's way of being in the world is beyond what you can have. You have to find your own way of being in the world.

It is difficult for all Fours to commit to more doing. Because of the way you see, your initial approach to a new idea or a new experience is to find the flaws. You do that because you don't want to be disappointed later, but what you imagine about what will be is very likely not true. Learning to allow the flaws to enter your thoughts and then set them aside lets you move forward. Who knows what the final outcome will be? You don't know and you can't know unless you follow through. All you have to do is begin.

Practice observing yourself nonjudgmentally.

It will also be helpful if Fours can admit that the repetitive pattern of feeling and thinking and feeling and thinking causes you problems because you ruminate on the wrong things. And while that is satisfying in some ways, it doesn't make life any better in the long run. Learn to break that pattern and focus on what you can do about whatever concerns you.

IT'S WORTH IT: DAVID'S STORY

As the head football coach of a new program at an academically elite Catholic college preparatory high school, we had a very limited talent pool of athletes. But I stepped into this role as an Enneagram Four with relative ease. The insurmountable odds provided an environment that matched my internal terrain—Fours know better than any the agony of "not measuring up." But I settled on the motto "Find a Way," which both reflected my Four search for what is missing and my acknowledgment of the reality of the school and the prospects for our success as a team.

Though I had plenty of Four self-drama in the way I took on the role, in bringing up doing I prided myself on showing up every day with a positive attitude. I really wanted to inspire all in the football program to believe we could be successful. Having surrendered to the reality of where I was, and the job that was mine to do, I found solace with the grind of the routine. It was a challenge, but over time alumni who played football for me have told me that my authenticity in accepting what the program really was and leading accordingly was an inspiration to them as players. And that made it so worth it for me.

TRY THIS

SOME TRANSFORMATIVE POSSIBILITIES

- The first step for every number is awareness. You can't change what you can't name. And you can't name the things you are unaware of. So, practice observing yourself nonjudgmentally. (When you judge yourself you defend yourself, and unfortunately that means more personality and less of who you really are.)

- Try making a list of all the things that you are really good at. Then add to it the lovely things that other people say about you. From there perhaps you can celebrate your way of being without feeling the need to be more like someone else.

- Recognize that the feeling that something is missing is a wake-up call for you. It means you are operating on autopilot and missing what is happening in the present moment.

- Be careful when you feel like you are different from everyone else. In that moment of awareness, stop and name what you have in common with others. Then focus on the gifts you have that make you unique in healthy and life-giving ways.

■ Become more aware of what causes your moods to change. You need to be self-aware enough to know where your focus is and where your attention naturally goes. What you focus on determines what you miss. So when you're focused on what's missing, you also miss your own gifts and graces.

■ Be careful about searching for intensity because of your aversion to things that are average and normal. This may be the primary reason you avoid doing. So much of what requires action is part of a routine. It is boring and dull, and tedious—and normal.

■ Work on focusing your attention on doing:

- Make it a priority.
- Plan your day, giving thought to details of what you will do.
- Recognize that the things you don't like to do still have to be done.
- Spend some of your energy wondering about what others need.
- Be careful with your neediness. You are perfectly able to manage the practical things in life.
- Let go of past hurts by seeking healing and practicing forgiveness.
- Pray for serenity, which is the quality or state of being calm and peaceful.

QUESTIONS TO PONDER

When you don't do your part of the day-to-day work and responsibility, how does it affect your relationships? Who does your part? How do they feel about it?

When you push people away who you really care about, what are you saying? Does push-pull really help the relationship? (I'm convinced that sometimes when Fours push-pull it is a substitute for doing what needs to be done.)

Could it be that you spend more energy avoiding something that needs to be done than the required energy to do it?

How often do you connect doing to your passion of envy? Do you make up stories about having to do things you don't want or like to do, imagining that others don't have such dreadful responsibilities?

What would it be like for you to use a mantra to help you stay focused on doing? For example, you can say to yourself while you wash the dishes or take out the trash or tend to the laundry: think and do. Think and do. Just think and do.

Fours have such deep and beautiful feelings. Those feelings are enhanced when you have feelings followed by the luxury of thinking about them. That will not be diminished when you work to add an appropriate amount of doing to your ways of being in the world. And you will find joy and beauty and surprise every single time you do what is yours to do, if you can be present to what is going on now and allow it to give you its gift. When that happens, you have what you need to gift the rest of us with descriptions of how you see the world, so we could perhaps enjoy, for just a moment, the beauty that you see.

5s

BE PRESENT TO THE WORLD

In Enneagram language, Fives are often called the Observer. This is because Fives interpret the world through the Thinking Center. The world outside of themselves is for gathering information, and they use logic coupled with what they already have filed away in their heads to assign value to the new data. Fives are most at home in their inner world of ideas, which means they can be withdrawn much of the time. Their approach to life is heady and feels somewhat disconnected because they tend to hoard knowledge. And when other people suggest ideas that are different from theirs, they usually stay silent while they are objecting and disagreeing inside.

I can't estimate how many thoughts Fives have that they don't share when in conversation with others because they are hesitant to tell me. I suspect it's a lot. They appear to feel vulnerable when they share what they think. And I would guess they don't want to argue or defend their conclusions because it would require energy that they would rather invest in some other way.

For many Fives, social connection is often perfunctory in part because they are so private. Most Fives tell me that they believe they are socially awkward, and added to that, being with people requires a lot of energy no matter what number you are. Imagine being a Five and having to manage the measured amount of energy that is yours every morning to use expeditiously through the day. And it's important to know that their time belongs to them. If you want some of it, they will determine the validity of your request. Our friends John and Carolyn have decided that their time with us is worth the expenditure of energy, yet they often say little at gatherings and often just watch all the goings on around them. But we have all learned that they are usually paying attention; if we want to hear from them, we can ask.

For Fives the support Center of Intelligence is feeling. They take in information with thinking, but they process it or make sense of it using both thinking and feeling. That suggests many things, but the most important might be that they are oriented toward what's going on inside of them. Fives' emotional energy is attached to their ideas. It's understandable that they would defend their own ideas because of the way they feel about them. Their knowledge is personal because it's *their* knowledge. Some numbers are name droppers, trying to impress others with who they know. Not Fives. They would much rather be associated with what they know. And when their ideas are misunderstood or rejected, they take it personally.

> Fives have to engage doing to move beyond planning to accomplishing.

Like Fours, Fives repress doing. Stamina and determination are lost in people who repress doing because both are a byproduct of that Center of Intelligence. That reality often leaves withdrawing numbers believing they can't affect the world or their environment. When that feels like a reality to Fives, all they are left with is their ideas. But those ideas—and the pursuit of information—are so important to them that they may actually drive them to more doing. Our friend John was at the forefront of treating Covid-19 patients in our area. In his Fiveness, he was trying to figure out the virus, so he was mentally charged, which allowed him to work long hours at the hospital. He didn't have much energy left over when he came home; he was saving it for his next shift.

Fives are generally invested in only doing what interests them. They ignore or don't even see other tasks that need to be done. They love to plan, and then refine their plans, and then think and rethink their plans. At times planning is so interesting and satisfying, the thing they're planning for never happens.

One of the reasons I've devoted much of my adult life to teaching the Enneagram is that while it points out many problems associated with our personalities, at the very same time it offers us a solution. For the numbers in the Withdrawing Stance, the problems are made easier when efforts are made to bring up the Doing Center, along with thinking and feeling. Life is so much better when we all make the effort to use all three Centers of Intelligence, each for its own purpose.

KEYS FOR FIVES TO BRING UP DOING

I applaud the way Fives value thinking. But it's important to consider that thinking can be used much more effectively if you are able to separate it from your feelings and when you also connect it to doing. The peace that you seek is only available if you find ways to balance thinking and feeling with some doing. It's a big struggle for you when you feel incapable or incompetent, so it will be very challenging for you to begin using the Center of Intelligence that you least favor and the one you employ with the least success. But if you practice using it, things will soon be measurably better.

The passion for Fives is avarice, which is usually defined as a greed for money. Fives may or may not struggle with that. But chances are you are greedy when it comes to time and space. And it's likely that your greed for knowledge plays a big role in your life every single day. It likely keeps you from doing. And that comes with consequences that you may not even be aware of. For example, Fives never reveal all they know, and they rarely disclose where they stand on any issue until it may be too late. When you behave in this way, you don't have the opportunity to learn from others and perhaps question some of your own thinking. And others don't have a chance to learn from how you see and what you think. Both could be mutually helpful and beneficial to your relationships.

And mutuality is key. Fives hate to divulge anything personal while preferring to gather personal information from the lives of friends and family and acquaintances. Learning to share who you are and some of the details of your

> For Fives the support Center of Intelligence is feeling. They take in information with thinking, but they process it or make sense of it using both thinking and feeling.

life will help you in building the kind of relationships you want. Friends exchange the stories that make up their lives, including the successes and the failures, both thoughts and feelings. And if properly used, the Feeling Center will be a big help in your discernment about what is yours to do or what you might offer to do in these relationships. When you don't need connection, there is a good chance that others who you care about do.

The combination of thinking (about ideas) supported by feeling (emotional attachment to those ideas) creates the illusion for Fives that you have managed to pull together and live by a personal belief system that you trust. That's not all bad. But our belief systems need to be reexamined from time to time. We all need to consider whether what we thought in our twenties still seems right in our forties. Systems of belief that are inflexible often cause pain in our lives and the lives of others, and result in unnecessary fragmentation in our relationships. Most ideas need to be reexamined as we age and grow, and we need to make room for changes in how we understand things, should that be necessary.

Fives have to engage doing to move beyond planning to accomplishing. And you will find great satisfaction when you participate in projects that make the world a better place for others rather than only focusing only on what interests you.

IT'S WORTH IT: TATE'S STORY

The hardest part for me in bringing up doing is remembering that I can't wait for motivation to change my behavior because, more often than not, the motivation just won't come. When the fact that I'm doing repressed totally takes over, I have to be really intentional about what I want to accomplish. I look for small tasks or behaviors that are relatively easy to finish, make a list of them, and then keep building on that. Even if a task isn't directly related to the areas of my life that I'm most passionate about, it still counts. When I'm done at the grocery store or finish folding my laundry, I try to take a moment to remind myself that, while this wasn't the sexiest or most significant of accomplishments, I still did something!

In relationships, I find that part of being thinking dominant is not wanting to speak or do until the thought or idea is fully formed. I realized this is dangerous because sometimes the "processing time" I need comes across as being disengaged or disinterested. I have learned to take a moment to remind myself that it's all right if I can't say exactly what I want to say in exactly the way I want to say it and that, at the very least, the person I'm with will appreciate knowing where I'm at in my process.

TRY THIS

SOME TRANSFORMATIVE POSSIBILITIES

■ Recognize that a scarcity mentality doesn't really help. You have enough energy to give to emotional connections, resolve conflicts, and finish projects. All these may very well *give* you energy rather than simply using it up.

■ Name the way your attention migrates to what you think other people are going to want or expect from you, and your assumption that it will intrude on your need for space and interfere with your agenda. If you can name that pattern, you can change it.

■ Notice when you are detaching from what's going on or when you are wanting to withdraw. Stop yourself and practice being present.

■ Recognize that your biggest challenge is connecting to the real world beyond the world in your head.

■ Be careful when you are minimizing your own needs. Sometimes when you are avoiding feeling responsible for meeting the needs of someone else, you don't take care of yourself either.

■ Recognize how and what you are hoarding: time, affection, things, resources, information, thoughts, even yourself. When it comes to your heart, the more you give the more you receive. Hoarding is particularly dangerous for Fives—it is a central way of withdrawing. Consider naming what you hoard and trying to convert that fear into generosity.

■ Be aware that people will not know what they mean to you unless you tell them.

- Be intentional about incorporating music, liturgy, and ritual into your life so that you are using all your senses as a way of bringing yourself out of your head.
- Pray to be more generous. The result will surprise you, leaving you with more than you gave, every single time.
- Learn to identify what circumstances make you the most uncomfortable in the world and consider what you can do or learn that would make you more comfortable.
- When others are honoring your need for time alone, give them a time when you will be available.

QUESTIONS TO PONDER

Is it possible to pause your personalization of everything and the way you cling to your point of view? Might there be other points of view that are valid?

How does it undermine your relationships with yourself and with others when you leave social responsibilities and initiatives up to them?

What values would you like to be remembered for at the end of your life?

What the world needs now, perhaps more than anything, is a gift that Fives carry without fanfare: neutrality. Do you know how rare it is for any of the rest of us to stumble on impartial space, where thinking forms ideas and opinions have little value? You are able to set the table for conversations that are unbiased, unprejudiced, and nonpartisan. It's a beautiful gift, and I'm thankful for every time you have the necessary energy to share it with the rest of us.

9s

MAKE A CHOICE—
YOU CAN CHANGE YOUR MIND

Nines interpret the world through the Doing Center, with their sense of what they should do, but they don't use doing to make sense of the information they receive. That is what makes them both doing dominant and doing repressed. Another way to think of this is that Nines make their way in the world using only part of the Doing Center. Keep in mind that the core numbers on the Enneagram—Three, Six, and Nine—are both dominant *and* repressed in the same Center of Intelligence.

Nines are part of the Withdrawing Stance and they are focused on trying to manage both internal and external boundaries. They try to keep in anything that might cause conflict, and they try to keep out anything that will rob them of their peace. And that is very tiring, so much so that Nines have the least energy of any number. That lack of energy is a big problem that complicates a Nine's ability to bring up repressed doing. As they manage those internal and external forces, they often have to withdraw in an effort to maintain some sense of protection. When outside pressure from not doing begins to build, Nines feel somewhat paralyzed. They lose their ability to see how they can affect the situation. Keep in mind that sloth, their Enneagram passion, has two aspects:

preferred doing makes action a value, and repressed doing makes action seem frivolous, useless, and even impossible.

Like other numbers, Nines process, or make sense of the information they absorb, using only two of the three centers. If thinking is dominant, feeling will support it, or if feeling is dominant, thinking will be in the supportive role. All to say, in terms of processing information, Nines decide how to respond to life with thinking and feeling but without consideration for doing.

That means they internalize information, and they value their interpretations. But they dismiss the value of acting on the information once it's been processed. In short, Nines take in information with what needs to be done, but it usually doesn't occur to them that they should actually *do* anything.

> Nines decide how to respond to life with thinking and feeling but without consideration for doing.

At our family gatherings, I have often observed that my husband, Joe, is happy to be there and to do all the barbequing, which he has always claimed as his job, but he seldom offers an opinion about the rest of the menu. And he prefers to let others intervene if two of the littles aren't getting along. This is safe space for Joe. The barbeque is always good, so he is in good shape there. And avoiding possible conflict with the littles is always a win for him.

It's very important to remember that Nines will do almost anything to avoid conflict. They learned at a young age to protect their peace and their safety by keeping their thoughts to themselves. Unfortunately, with repressed doing, their determination to maintain that inner peace can become stubbornness. In fact, Nines are the most stubborn number on the Enneagram. But that stubbornness almost always involves *doing* (or a lack thereof).

Support center. The support of thinking and feeling makes Nines competent in complex situations. They frequently offer enlightened solutions to problems. We sometimes fail to notice their gifts because Nines don't stand out and they don't want to stand out. They are open to the thoughts and feelings of others because their way of seeing is to acknowledge that there are at least two sides to everything. Nines are slow and steady and determined, but they benefit from collaboration with others in figuring out what needs to be done.

Nines are easily distracted, so even when they are doing what needs to be done, they could quickly switch to something else in the middle of the process. Our Nine daughter Jenny used to tell me that cleaning the house when her children were little was only possible if she put something in front of the door to remind her to finish the room she was in before following a distraction that led her to another part of the house.

KEYS FOR NINES TO BRINGING UP DOING

The first step for Nines is cultivating awareness of their behavior. That will be a challenge because it takes a lot of energy to be self-aware and then even more energy to do something about what you discover. When you observe yourself, notice how often you choose not to say something that you believe could cause fragmentation. One reason Nines struggle with doing lies in the reality that they often avoid speaking up when decisions are being made about what could or should be done. From their perspective other voices seem louder and more convincing, so they set aside their thoughts or desires or plans in the process of going along with stronger personalities. They succeed in avoiding conflict with this decision. But they lose their focus, and their plans for doing are once again thwarted.

Later is not a point in time! Understanding and accepting this reality is almost as important as awareness. Nines tend to think they are making a commitment when they say to others or to themselves, "I'll do that later." Most of the time, later doesn't come because there are so many distractions and other things to tend to. Trust this: the peace you love so much will come much sooner—and last much longer—as a result of engaging and doing.

> The peace you love so much will come much sooner—and last much longer—as a result of engaging and doing.

For each of the numbers who are doing repressed, certain things necessary for living an intentional life are lost. Assertiveness is learned through doing, and we've learned from Don Riso and Russ Hudson that the unconscious childhood message for Nines is "It's not okay to assert yourself." But it is okay. Part of your work and responsibility is to overcome this message and find a way to make your thoughts and desires known to others, even those who might disagree.

IT'S WORTH IT: REES'S STORY

One of the biggest challenges for me is to actually start something. (I have a pretty strong One wing, which allows me to put off acting until I can do something perfectly.) This past year, I adopted the word advocate *as my watchword. I was determined to be an advocate for myself in work, church, and family situations. That meant that I needed to "show up" more often and be present. I also vowed to advocate for others when it was necessary. This was and continues to be a challenge for me, and I haven't always stepped up to the challenge. But the times when I have "entered the fray" have been very enlightening and encouraging—and never as difficult as I imagined. And even when my suggestions haven't been followed, simply joining the conversation has been huge for me.*

TRY THIS

SOME TRANSFORMATIVE POSSIBILITIES

■ Take time to recharge and spend some free time alone to prepare yourself for being present to all the things that make up your life. Most Nines love nature, perhaps because there is no pressure there. A good spiritual practice would be spending planned time, with appropriate boundaries, out in nature every week. Many Nines have shared with me that it feels very selfish to take a whole day to do whatever they want to do. There are seasons of life when an entire day is acceptable, and in other seasons a half day will do.

■ Recognize that "all things are equal" or "if left alone, most things work themselves out" is often not the case. These are representative of what you tell yourself because of your strong desire to avoid conflict and because of repressed doing. What would change if you stopped using these sayings to support your lack of involvement?

■ Please consider giving up your tendency to erase yourself and choose participation instead.

■ Set some goals for yourself—things you really want to do. Then share them, one at a time, with someone you trust and ask them to hold you accountable. Meeting with them regularly will be helpful.

■ Pray for diligence. It is life-giving when you intentionally pursue both your personal and professional goals.

■ Spend some time thinking about your significant relationships. Identify two or three specific things you could do to let these people know how much they mean to you and how grateful you are for their presence in your life.

■ Try becoming aware of the daily, weekly, monthly, regular, and irregular but ordinary tasks that surround you.
Then do them without being asked or reminded.

QUESTIONS TO PONDER

*What tasks in your personal life are you avoiding? If you completed them,
how would your life and your relationships improve?*

*What would happen if you decided to make a decision and take a
stand? You can always change your mind.*

*Think about the ways you tend to undervalue and disregard yourself.
How do you do that? What do you gain? What do you lose?*

*Could you develop a plan for allowing pain from your past to fall
away? You might be surprised with the energy that is the result of
letting go.*

Nines are well loved. I think sometimes people envy your peacefulness, but of course they have no idea what you have to do to
protect it. The Nines in our family are deeply respected, not just by
us but by their friends and coworkers as well. We appreciate the
gift you have for seeing two sides to everything and the way it
equips you for mediation between people who want to get along
but can't—as our Nines have done from time to time for us. You
are thoughtful and loyal and treasured by almost all of the people
who know you. It's heartbreaking when you think you are unimportant or that what you offer is something anyone else could have
contributed. Your presence matters. And if you don't remember
anything else from this chapter, please remember that.

CHAPTER FIVE

THE AGGRESSIVE STANCE

STANDING INDEPENDENTLY

As an Enneagram teacher, I am sometimes asked to teach "Know Your Enneagram Number" to church staffs to help them work together better. Churches are much like other organizations; the same interpersonal dynamics often are at work, so the Enneagram can be valuable in helping everyone understand why they behave as they do.

That was true at one vibrant church I visited known for its creative programs that run smoothly and have been copied by other churches who hope for equal success. They are committed to serving all ages, and they work to make space for cultural difference. Their leadership team is made up of three people who are all in the Aggressive Stance. This means all three repress feeling, but that takes a distinctive shape for each of them.

After the general session, I decided to talk to the staff and see what they had observed about each other. Elaine, the administrative assistant, told me that she enjoyed working for David, the senior pastor, who is a Seven. She admired the way he had grown the church during his tenure and smiled as she shared that he is well loved by most and tolerated by others. From the general session, Elaine knew that Sevens are typically energetic and charming, and told me that he is both. And, she added, he is smart and creative and throws out ideas faster than people in a staff meeting can write them down. She said she often wondered if he had any limits.

David seemed to like lots of stimulation (as is typical for Sevens), and he loved nothing more than new ideas, especially if he knew his staff could potentially turn them into reality. Elaine also told me that the other two pastors sometimes complained to her that they aren't sure what to do with all of David's ideas but that over time they have learned that he is exploring and imagining all the time, so they wait to join him until he eventually "lands" on one idea that stands out above the rest. Elaine continued, saying that one of them said, "If David hasn't said it three times, we're not going to do anything to move forward with one of his ideas."

> Perhaps the biggest problem associated with repressed feelings is that these numbers give up some of their ability to be touched and affected by life.

After Elaine, I walked down the hallway to talk to Marilyn, an associate pastor in her fifties, who has been at the church for six years, which is two years longer than David. She confirmed Elaine's take on David's energy and said she liked his vision for the church, but as an Enneagram Three she worried about being successful in her work when there are so many moving parts, and suggestions for creative change often surface before an existing program has had a chance to prove its effectiveness.

As Marilyn described her many duties, it seemed to me she was perfectly suited to handling them all. She said she loved meeting with wedding couples to prepare them for marriage and plan their ceremony. She liked the combination of being a good listener and a wise counselor while sharing their excitement about the many details that go into making their special day. She said she felt honored to be the one to visit hospitals and retirement homes where she could share in the pain of an elder's loneliness, or sit with an unexpected diagnosis or the sadness of approaching the end of life. She often had to both officiate a wedding and visit a hospital in the same day but seemed surprised when I asked her if that was hard. In fact, she told me, that was one of her strengths, as was her ability to move back and forth between the traditional and contemporary services on Sunday mornings. She seemed to be just what everyone wanted in a pastor. As we talked, I thought about the fact that the best part of every number is also the worst. For Marilyn, the best part of Three is that she can become whatever her audience will accept and approve. But that is also the worst part because her behavior is somewhat different depending on who she is with. It makes it challenging for people who are with Marilyn day in and day out to know which Marilyn they will encounter.

When I talked to David, he had told me he is a little envious of Marilyn's flexibility and the joy she finds in all of her responsibilities. He said he likes working with couples who are planning for their weddings but finds hospital visits difficult, and isn't really comfortable dealing with grief and planning for funeral services. He asked me lots of questions about the difference between being flexible and being an agent for change, which in his mind ensured growth. I was pleased to see that he could recognize that while he really likes to be part of new and exciting things, he is not particularly flexible.

The last of my conversations was with Elizabeth, an Eight who is the associate pastor in charge of programming. Elizabeth told me she prefers to be given a project and then left alone. She was up-front about her need to be in charge. Her manner in our conversation was blunt, direct, and straightforward but friendly. She told me she prefers to evaluate a plan, assign the responsibilities, work hard, do everything well, finish, and then measure its value to the congregation. She said she may tweak something from time to time, but if it works, she has no desire to change it. I already knew from my other conversations with her colleagues that the programs in the church that fall under her purview run smoothly, so her approach was working. I could see that *she differs from David in that she gets her energy from precision and success, while he is energized by spontaneity and change.*

After these conversations, I had some insights into the team. I could see that Elizabeth differs from Marilyn because as an Eight, she is not motivated by feelings, hers or anyone else's. Marilyn, in her Threeness, is both feeling dominant and feeling repressed. That means she takes in information from the environment with feelings but then she doesn't let those feelings determine what she will do. For Elizabeth, awareness of others' feelings may influence her methods, but it will seldom, if ever, change her plan. She doesn't need approval or accolades from others. She is unapologetically powerful, and I was glad to see that David has learned to challenge her when absolutely necessary but otherwise lets her operate independently.

When I talked with David, it was clear to me that he is learning to be in the leadership position with both Marilyn and Elizabeth, and the Enneagram is helping. He understands that Elizabeth as an Eight is either all in, or not in at all—regardless of what is being considered. She has very definite ideas about what to have for lunch and how to fund next year's mission trip and everything in between. David knows he can match her energy but not her relentlessness. Marilyn doesn't try. David avoids confrontation, but he isn't afraid of it. Marilyn doesn't like relationship trouble of any kind, but she doesn't run from it. And Elizabeth finds confrontation to be energizing. As a group of aggressive numbers, they are finding their way.

THE THREE REALITIES OF REPRESSED FEELING

Over the years, I've observed that aggressive numbers like to work with other aggressive numbers. My latest thinking about why that's true is that Threes, Sevens, and Eights think faster than the rest of us and that energizes all of them. They are also feeling repressed. If we can imagine a world where there are no feelings to be dealt with, apologized for, managed, or accommodated—and that's what these aggressive numbers would like—it would be fast paced, exciting, full of possibility, and known for all that is accomplished. Of course, there are a lot of valuable things missing in this alternative reality. But getting things done is not one of them. Threes, Sevens, and Eights appreciate the momentum and the lack of personal exchange and involvement, and they are comforted by the fact that they can accomplish a lot—and quickly. They are colleagues and therefore collegial, but they are not usually friends.

David as a Seven, Marilyn as a Three, and Elizabeth as an Eight are all in the Aggressive Stance: all leave out feeling while relying on thinking and doing.

- As one of the core numbers on the Enneagram, Threes are both feeling dominant and feeling repressed. As a result, either thinking or doing will dominate the way Threes make sense of things. One will lead and the other will support.

- For Sevens, thinking is dominant and doing supports thinking, meaning they take in information using thinking, and then they make sense of it using thinking and doing.

- For Eights, doing is dominant and thinking supports doing, meaning they take in information using the Doing Center and then they make sense of it using doing and thinking.

Aggressive in relation to stances refers to these numbers' unconscious drive to reshape people and situations the way they

THE AGRESSIVE STANCE

NUMBER	TRIAD	STANCE	PREFERRED AND DOMINANT CENTER	SUPPORT CENTER	REPRESSED CENTER
Three	Heart	Aggressive	Feeling	Thinking / Doing Doing / Thinking	Feeling
Seven	Head	Aggressive	Thinking	Doing	Feeling
Eight	Gut	Aggressive	Doing	Thinking	Feeling

want them to be. Threes, Sevens, and Eights stand independently, in contrast to the Withdrawing Stance where the move is away from others. Those in the Aggressive Stance determine how they will use their energy, and they push back against getting tangled up in the personal stuff of life. They are focused on controlling their environment while accomplishing their tasks and achieving their goals.

All three personality types leave out the Feeling Center. They dismiss the importance of emotions, interpersonal dynamics, and other people's agendas. Perhaps the biggest problem associated with repressed feelings is that these numbers give up some of their ability to be touched and affected by life. To be clear, all three have feelings and emotions, but they choose to express them indirectly. They aren't emotional because they dismiss emotions as an interruption in the more important things that require their attention.

> Threes, Sevens, and Eights are heavily focused on "what is about to happen," as their orientation to time is the future.

Those of us who are not in this stance struggle to understand aggressive numbers primarily because they seldom share how they feel.

Over the years, people who are in this stance have told me that they don't have the vocabulary to express feelings. They consistently dodge personal questions, but you might not notice it until the conversation is over. Those who are in relationship with Threes, Sevens, and Eights see this lack of vocabulary as a missed opportunity. But for them, it protects their privacy, avoids expectations from others, and increases their sense of personal freedom. In addition, none of them like surprises or unexpected emotions. They find both to be disquieting and off-putting because feelings of vulnerability are not normal for this stance.

It takes some time to get to know and understand how aggressive numbers see the world. When I was first learning the Enneagram, maybe six years into the process, I was more surprised by these three numbers than any others. Just when I thought I had them figured out, I didn't. They are very tender but find feelings to be messy and unpredictable. They respond to the needs of others with action instead of feelings, but they respond. Threes believe feelings block efficiency. Sevens find feelings to be limited to what's happening in the present moment when the future is right around the corner. And Eights substitute lust, which is their passion, for all of the other feelings unless something striking or unpredicted happens.

Threes, Sevens, and Eights are heavily focused on what is about to happen, as their orientation to time is the future. That may be productive for doing, but being tethered to the future also offers a disguise for their weakness when it comes to forming personal relationships. They don't need to relate to others in situations that don't yet exist. And they avoid what they would call unnecessary vulnerability.

The Aggressive Stance's Orientation to Time

Threes, Sevens, and Eights are heavily focused on "what is about to happen," since their orientation to time is the future:

- Threes prefer to focus on completing the next project and the goals they have identified beyond that.
- A Seven's attention is almost always looking toward the future; much of life's joy is in anticipation.
- Eights are problem solving their future crises or struggles. Most of the time, Eights have already identified potential problems and determined their solutions before they occur.

The people in the Aggressive Stance get your attention. They all have lots of energy; they're active and vital and very determined. They are big picture thinkers who usually have a full schedule and lots to attend to. While they don't naturally or intuitively connect to feelings, theirs or others', they do spot trouble, and they handle it. And as part of all of this, they have lots of ideas about how the world should be, and they try to turn those ideas into reality. Life for Threes, Sevens, and Eights is about control, and most have shared with me that wanting to be in charge began when they were young.

All three personality types have told me repeatedly that they are often the ones who provide the energy for many of the groups they belong to. They quickly add that sometimes it feels like a burden. They think other people move too slow, and they have some impatience with that, but they tend to avoid addressing it directly. I've heard lots of stories about times when people in this stance decided to make an effort to be seen but not heard, or to hang back in a meeting or at a social event. Frequently the story ends with someone else coming to them, encouraging them to step forward or speak up.

3s

I AM MORE THAN WHAT I DO

Threes like Marilyn in our opening story see and interpret the world through the Feeling Center. But they don't use feelings to process or make sense of the information they have received. *Preferring* feeling means they are fully aware of other people's expressed emotions, needs, motives, and expectations, but then they set that awareness aside and process information with thinking and doing. That's what enables Marilyn to be with wedding couples and make hospital visits—she senses their emotions but does not let them affect her. Like other Threes, Marilyn is outwardly personable but inwardly distant and impersonal. She is taking in information from her environment using feeling, but then she sets those feelings aside and focuses on thinking and doing.

This is an important element for understanding the Enneagram: the way we make sense of things determines our worldview, and our worldview is the basis for our actions. The three Centers of Intelligence are our natural resources. Many of our successes, and failures, can be explained by understanding that, for the most part, we primarily use two of the three.

For Threes, either thinking or doing may be dominant, but they act together and orient them toward work. Threes like Marilyn focus their attention on their own ideas and their own actions. In work settings, they plan projects (thinking) and then complete them (doing). That's partly why they are so successful.

In fact, the Three's best strengths come from thinking and doing regardless of which one is dominant. They process information quickly and are gifted problem-solvers. They communicate well and get along with most people. Their ability to set aside differences or misunderstandings while working with others toward a common goal is a great gift. And when they're healthy or even in average space, people tend to really like them.

It can be considered a gift for Threes that they are both feeling dominant and feeling repressed. The Feeling Center's capacity for being aware of and responding to people's feelings is the basis for a Three's ability to begin building relationships before they rely solely on the other two centers. And those relationships are one of the biggest reasons why someone like Marilyn has enjoyed so much professional success in her work at her church.

> A key to change is to begin to observe how much you value efficiency and effectiveness.

But because the Feeling Center is repressed and not used when making sense of the world, the Three's interest in relationships is often superficial. They manage by mechanically responding to the world, carefully managing words and actions in ways that have the potential to get the best response from others. Threes are all about productivity, and they tell me that relationships are time-consuming and that when people are needy, they struggle to know how to respond. My friend Brock summarized the way this feels for Threes:

Being a Three, it's a bit tricky for my dominant center to also be my repressed center. My Three feeling dominance is about scanning the room for people or situations to ultimately learn what these folks find to be successful. It's as if my Feeling Center only extends about halfway to another person, not fully looking to connect, but looking to gain information on what to do or how to think in order to be viewed as "successful." It's a way of getting information via the Feeling Center, but not using the Feeling Center to respond to that information.

It's important to remember that while taking in information with the Feeling Center is helpful, repressed feeling causes Threes to become bored and impatient with the expression of feelings in others. Marilyn, for example, may cut her meetings short if a situation becomes emotionally charged. Threes struggle to share their own feelings and emotions, but early in a relationship people often miss that because of their polished presentation of both social and professional charm and confidence.

KEYS FOR THREES TO BRING UP FEELING

It's hard to accept that none of us can change how we see. But we can change what we do with how we see.

One of the most valuable insights I've learned from Threes over the years is that they overvalue efficiency. And Threes who are serious about a journey toward transformation would do well to begin with embracing the reality that efficiency may be their Achilles' heel. That's why a key to change is to begin to observe how much you value efficiency and effectiveness. Both have value in their place and in right relationship to every other measure of success, whether when evaluating a project or in a relationship, but they are not always the most important.

Threes will have to slow down to learn to be good at self-observation and take note of behavior that you hope to change without judging yourself. Remember that it is your personality that judges and your personality that defends. All to say, your Threeness will just get bigger and bigger, and who you are underneath all of that will continue to be obscured unless you cultivate greater self-awareness.

Almost everyone—including Threes—misunderstands the Three's passion, which is deceit. It will be almost impossible to bring up feelings if the Enneagram meaning of deceit is not known and understood. A Three's deceit is rarely an intentional lie. Instead, deceit occurs when Threes become over identified with the images they have crafted and presented in order to make their way in the world. Keep in mind that their motivation from the beginning is to give other people what they want. But Threes get caught in image crafting, and they begin to believe that they are only their external selves. They fear that when they look inside there will be nothing there. That is not true. And they have to get over that obstacle if they are going to be able to access and name their real feelings and desires. And that is followed by committing to bring up those real feelings in an effort to achieve balance by appropriately using all three Centers of Intelligence.

Threes will need to gradually, over time, become more consistent in their efforts to rely less and less on image crafting and habitual behavior, and more on their own enlightened understanding of using all three centers in a healthy and balanced way. And it's important to keep in mind that all the numbers, not just Threes, have to work to have less personality and more of their essential nature.

IT'S WORTH IT: REBECCA'S STORY

I like to say that being feeling repressed and feeling dominant is like standing in the shallowness of a baby pool. You're in water, but it's just a couple inches before you hit the bottom. For me as a Three, feelings are always right there at the surface—those few inches of water. I can sense them all around me, and I can sense them in other people. It's like the feelings are hiding in plain sight—in a sad commercial or in the kind words of a friend—just waiting for me to feel them. And I do! I feel them for a moment. But I feel them with the depth of the baby pool—a quick tear falls or a fleeting joy swells. And then, the moment is over, and I pack the feelings away, nice and tidy and back on the shelf.

My transactions with feelings are brief, cursory even. So, when my mom had a second cancer diagnosis—metastatic this time—and I entered a prolonged season of deep feeling, I became a foreigner to myself. Feelings were everywhere and in everything. Just crossing the threshold of my mother's house undid me. Talking to my friends made me weep. I couldn't speak about her or the state of our family without a cascade of feelings—sorrow, fear, sadness—that could not be swallowed and most assuredly could not be shelved. For the first time, perhaps, I was in the deep end of the pool and I was drowning in my feelings.

It's clear I've lived a sheltered life, one relatively untouched by the many griefs, assaults, and anxieties most of the world endures. I think I've always known that, but after my mother's diagnosis I realized I had so few tools to manage these dark seasons. I remember very little from that time, but I do remember a sobering conversation with my husband, Chris, my anchor, my Nine, who told me, "All feelings are for feeling. Let them come, listen to them, and then let them go. They don't want to stay forever." I think that was one of my greatest fears: that the bad feelings would stay forever. That I would be miserable forever, and that I would be seen as someone who couldn't keep her stuff together. My relationship to feelings is as much about my outward management of my appearance as it is my inward management of a complex and occasionally perplexing inner life. But as Chris chided me to remember (and as a therapist, helped me accomplish), I tried to just feel my feelings. I tried not to manage them, nor forget them. It was intentional and it was terrifying.

TRY THIS

SOME TRANSFORMATIVE POSSIBILITIES

- Work on being aware of all the steps involved in creating the "image" that you believe will make you the person other people expect or want you to be.

- Learn to separate thinking and doing so that each one's agenda will be well developed. When that happens, it is much easier to bring up feeling. It might help to:

  - Use thinking to ponder the deeper meaning of things and be creative in contributing to the greater good of your community.

  - Notice how the combination of thinking and doing can seduce you into believing that the impersonal is more important than the personal.

  - Try using the Doing Center to *stop*. You usually do too much and enjoy it too little.

  - Use thinking in areas other than goal setting and achieving.

  - Pay attention to this cyclical pattern: thinking → planning → doing → accomplishing → thinking, and so on. It is the origin of your excessive focus on work.

- In observing yourself, try to identify parts of your way of being in the world that stay the same no matter who you're with or what you're doing. You can learn to use that behavior as the baseline for establishing the person you are, without crafting an image you think others would prefer.

- You're not going to like this one at first, but if you will try it for six months, you will very likely change your mind: make time every day for some kind of contemplative practice.

■ Notice that as you grow in your ability to bring up feelings, you will find time with others more rewarding and time alone more fulfilling.

■ Invest in being as emotionally vulnerable as you can, and be sure you order your life in ways that allow you to spend time alone. Both will be of great benefit.

■ Try out some artistic pursuits that use a part of your brain that is different from the thinking, planning, and doing wheel of your activity.

■ See if you can make room in your life for some journaling. (Feel free to ask someone you trust to dispose of your journals should anything happen to you.) Some suggestions for topics for journaling:

- Why do you remain silent about things in your heart you know you need to share?

- Why do you resist making time in your life for spiritual or contemplative work?

- What specific kinds of information do you withhold? Why?

- Value yourself for who you are instead of what you do.

QUESTIONS TO PONDER

How can you create some space, maybe every other day, for naming your own feelings and needs? Then share one of them with someone you trust.

What responsibilities can you hand off to someone else when you think you're the only one who can handle them? Don't start with something big because you might be right. But you also might be surprised.

What would it be like to be personal along with being personable in your relationships? I'm aware that being personable feels safe and it generally works for you. The problem is that it makes your personality bigger and your true self smaller.

It's very difficult to give up what works in the hopes that something different could be better. And your way of being in the world is probably very successful. I would suggest that your life might be more enjoyable and equally successful if you seek and then find more balance. Integrity, meaning being complete or undivided, is a goal for all of us, but it is the desired virtue for Threes.

> For Threes, either thinking or doing may be dominant, but they act together and orient them toward work.

My students and other people who share this Enneagram number tell me that working toward balancing the three Centers of Intelligence while also trying to balance work, rest, and play, along with the addition of a regular spiritual practice, makes a welcome difference in their lives. It sounds like a lot because it is, but you are accustomed to handling a challenge like this and much more.

7s

ALL FEELINGS MATTER

As a Seven, David, the senior pastor in our story, sees and interprets the world through the Thinking Center. He is keenly focused on information and logic, seeking out patterns and where they overlap. He finds it all exciting, and he is always thinking about what comes next or what he plans to do tomorrow. But he is less aware that even when those plans are positive and exciting, they are still temporary because like all Sevens he tends to keep his options open, ever aware that something better could come along at any time. Initiating new plans comes naturally to him, sometimes so much so that the rest of his staff feels left behind.

The support Center of Intelligence for Sevens is doing. That essentially means that they make sense of life with the combination of thinking and doing. And they experience a lot of freedom because they are oriented toward their own actions and experiences. They're active, energetic, and spontaneous. In fact, spontaneity is an absolute requirement in any relationship with a Seven. They are easygoing and keep in touch with lots of people, probably because they're among the most loyal types on the Enneagram. And although they prefer loose attachments, once they're committed to someone, they are deeply committed.

Because Sevens repress feeling, they dismiss the importance of emotions in themselves and in others, which may lead at times to dealing with relationships superficially. But they are also playful, and they find joy in being with people. Others (for example, David's staff) really enjoy being with them, which Sevens may not realize is different from having depth and richness in their emotional life.

Sevens are often surprised to learn that they repress feelings because they think they have so many. In considering a full range of emotions from happy to sad, Sevens are in tune with the happy feelings and ignore feelings that are unhappy. Their charm has served them well from an early age, as does their tenacity. If they want something from you, it's easier to just give in. I can testify to that because I have a Seven in my family, and, honestly, it's like being pecked to death by chickens. Their charm is seductive, and their humor is usually irresistible. When we find ourselves giving into their demands, it almost feels like we're doing the right thing. It's a challenge to love and care about Sevens enough to tell them no.

> For Sevens, the dreaming is essential. Sevens are often surprised to learn that they repress feelings because they think they have so many.

For Sevens, having and keeping a positive attitude while looking forward to all of the possibilities the future holds seems to be as vital to life as breathing. They often lead with humor, but it's primarily because it's expected. They have so much more to offer, and they genuinely hope they will have opportunities to share their intellectual and emotional depth.

Sevens protect their freedom in part by evaluating each opportunity that comes their way and then choosing what pleases them. I think it's because putting boundaries around their personal freedom is an outward expression of the internal reality that they are protecting themselves from feelings such as sadness, regret, loneliness, and even anger.

With every morning cup of coffee or tea, a new list emerges and expands in response to the Seven's imagination. Our son Joel is a Seven, so I've been aware of his dreams and supportive of his imagination all of his life. He works with us in Life in the Trinity Ministry and often travels with me. We were headed home from a weekend of teaching in Louisiana, about a three-hour drive, when Joel shared with me that he was planning to buy a motorcycle.

My willingness to listen was equally balanced by my obvious

> The support Center of Intelligence for Sevens is doing. That essentially means that they make sense of life with the combination of thinking and doing.

lack of support. Both my dad and my brother were doctors, and they had very strong feelings about the danger of motorcycles. They insisted when our boys were little that we do all we could to see to it that they never had one. I reminded Joel of their concerns, and ours, but parenting adult children is one of life's greatest challenges. Joel was not deterred. In fact, his excitement never waned. He told me the color of the bike, his destination and plan for his first road trip, and he included what he would be wearing from his helmet to boots.

Sevens dream of many things that will not become reality, and even if they do, the real thing never lives up to their expectations. But *the dreaming is essential.* Without it, daily life would be almost unbearable for Sevens. So those of us who love Sevens have to learn to weigh in at appropriate times, with the awareness that most of the things they imagine don't come to fruition and that part of the joy is in the dreaming.

KEYS FOR SEVENS TO BRING UP FEELING

Transformation begins when Sevens can separate thinking from doing. The pattern of thinking and doing and thinking and doing is limiting because self-awareness is unlikely. When things don't go well, it's usually a surprise to Sevens, who are in a rhythm that feels satisfying and life-giving and safe. Unfortunately, when you repress your own feelings, you also treat others' feelings as unimportant. If you can separate the centers and employ all three, while intentionally allowing for both introspection and increased awareness of others, you may discover that other people you love and care about don't necessarily share the feelings you're having. And in valuing their feelings, you may also uncover some of your own, both good and bad.

Aggressive numbers think fast—much faster than other Enneagram numbers. Keeping up is a challenge for the rest of us, while staying present to a single thought or idea is difficult for them. Admittedly that can be really helpful at times, but when Sevens hurry to act on what they're thinking about, it can be the first step in an escape plan that is usually triggered by the fear of anxiety or pain. That could become a necessary wake-up call for Sevens.

There is a tendency in Sevens, when they're in average or unhealthy space, to join doing with thinking to support curiosity and sometimes entitlement. When that happens without at least tipping your hat to feelings, purposefulness is usually missing. That's an important point because action without a purpose is often selfish, exclusive, or a waste of time.

The Seven passion, which is gluttony, is tricky. More than enough of almost anything is usually satisfying until it isn't. And then it's too late. Sevens, using preferred thinking, can imagine and plan endlessly, even to excess. And with the energy supply that is common to this number, they can execute many of their plans. But the question is whether they should. That's a deeper question to be considered about living at a slower pace, utilizing the gifts of all three Centers of Intelligence. If they don't bring up feelings, they will find that other people's agendas matter very little, and that will result in relationship problems that they don't want if they don't do something about it.

IT'S WORTH IT: JOEL'S STORY

When I was younger, I think I intuitively surrounded myself with head and gut people and avoided feeling people. It seemed a lot easier to maintain relationships that way, but it was also boring. That's one of the reasons my relationship with my wife, Whitney, is so great. She's a One. It took me a while to understand and then learn that I can't meet her emotions with my thinking. And she understands that she can't meet my thinking with her emotions. When we have a disagreement or end up in an argument, I can explain to her until the end of time why logically she is not making sense. And she can repeat over and over, "This is how I feel," or "Can you understand where I'm coming from?" Honestly, I still have to tell myself almost every day that I can't use thinking to make sense of feelings. Because frankly, they often don't make sense. Thinking can be right or wrong, logical or illogical, but feelings have no moral value. They just are.

Because of the Enneagram I am learning to include feelings in how I process information. They may not be my feelings. It's more about my growing ability to allow and acknowledge feelings in other people. When I can do that, I can sit with Whitney and understand that there are times when I feel things about myself and other people that aren't necessarily true. Only then can I relate honestly to Whitney's feelings and communicate with her without relying on thinking and logic because those don't meet her needs.

TRY THIS

SOME TRANSFORMATIVE POSSIBILITIES

■ Intentionally bring up feeling because you don't move there intuitively. Your wings are in thinking (Six) and doing (Eight). In stress you go to doing (One); in security you go to thinking (Five). There is no natural access to feeling if you don't make an effort to include it and develop it.

■ When tempted to escape a situation, stop before you redirect your attention and your energy, and ask yourself what happened and why you feel a need to transition to something else. When the desire to do something else is sudden, you can be sure that your personality is on autopilot and you are anxious or afraid.

■ Recognize that your ability to reframe any negative into a positive in an instant is not helpful. Everything has two sides, and Sevens tend to be unaware of the downsides. Even if you don't react to a situation, that doesn't mean it doesn't affect you.

■ Consider this: default programming keeps you in a half range of feelings. Perhaps you could trick your own personality by acknowledging that you don't want to miss anything, that is, the other half of available feelings and emotions. It will really help you with self-awareness, communication, and relations with other people.

■ Seek the virtue of humility and take responsibility for things on your side of the fence without having to be coached by others who are involved. Remember, it's a challenge for you to avoid reframing and acknowledge that there is a problem. And then, on top of that, it's hard for you to own your part in things. Your fear that unwanted pain will increase if you do own your part is not realistic. Actually, it's the other way around.

■ Choose quality over quantity. For example, a Seven could be intrigued by living in a four-thousand-square-foot house or a tiny home. Each would be satisfying in its own way. But over time, quantity requires too much of your freedom, and a tiny home would enhance it.

■ Pay attention when you're doing whatever will make your life easier because it may not end up being easier in the long run. Sometimes the longer journey is more rewarding.

■ Spend some time thinking about opening your heart—but not just when you choose and not just to certain people. You may have a significant amount of repressed sadness and regret. Both are very heavy to carry, but you can't address either one without bringing up the Feeling Center.

■ Consider spending time in silence. You tend to treat yourself to too much external stimulation. Begin by reading about silence as a spiritual practice, then set aside a time every day for silence, which, by the way, isn't just the absence of noise. In committing to this practice, you will learn to trust yourself in new ways, and you will find a new benchmark in what satisfies you.

■ Make sure that what you think you want in the moment will be good for you in the long run. It's a big temptation for you to go after something without considering the consequences.

■ Be careful with your focus on the future. It gives you the illusion of being free of difficulties and problems in the present.

■ Remember: it is not your job to keep yourself or other people "up" all the time.

QUESTIONS TO PONDER

What if happiness is a byproduct? What happens if you pay attention to the result when you go after happiness? Explore the times when happiness comes your way as a result of something else.

If you are an extroverted Seven, what would it be like if you talked less and learned to listen without interrupting? If you are an introverted Seven, how can you learn to stay mentally present to conversations?

What is one essential area of your life that most needs your attention? What two things could you do to improve the situation?

Consider some of the characteristics or behavior in other people that cause you to feel angry or impatient. Are these some of the things that you do too?

Enneagram wisdom suggests that Sevens need fortitude, which Merriam Webster defines as "strength of mind that enables a person to encounter danger or bear pain or adversity with courage." That doesn't mean that Sevens are not courageous or cannot handle adversity. It does mean that you use a smokescreen of activity to avoid the things you're afraid of. Be careful with that because your primary fear is the feelings on the sad end of the spectrum. As humans we will forever be confronted with fear and loss and sadness. As a Seven, you can successfully reframe all three, but reframing postpones more than it changes. Learn to stay present to what you would call negative emotions as they arise because what you don't grieve in the present moment, you will have to acknowledge and grieve in the future.

8s

VULNERABILITY IS NOT WEAKNESS

Like others in the Aggressive Stance, Eights such as Elizabeth in our opening story see and interpret the world through the Doing Center. In fact, more than any other number, they are focused on doing: either moving or sleeping, either all in or not in at all. Eights have so much energy that waiting for people to catch up—like Elizabeth's colleagues, David and Marilyn—feels like a colossal waste of time. Both of them told me that they sometimes felt her impatience with their questions. Determination is second nature to Eights, and it supports their strong desire to maintain personal power and control.

When I'm teaching, Eights are the people in the room who don't nod their heads in agreement when I insist that control is an illusion. When given an opportunity, they tell me that control—of people, personal space, and their own vulnerability—is essential, and they believe they can do that. They are determined to control the whole scene, not just parts. It's helpful to them to think that way because it depersonalizes actions that others may take personally.

If I ask the participants in an Enneagram workshop to write down what they are afraid of, some leave their pages blank and others claim they fear nothing at all. Eights think they are so strong and capable. However, if they grow in awareness, they discover that they are consistently afraid of betrayal and the vulnerability it exposes. Their solution is to stay vigilant in determining who is for them and who is against them.

Eights are relentless advocates for people who are powerless, using the same strength and discipline that they use to protect themselves. Perhaps their awareness of those who are marginalized in one way or another is intuitive because it is unlikely that it would come from the Feeling Center. Feelings might or might not be involved—it's their impulse to act that leads them to believe they can address injustice by doing something about it. They focus on doing the right thing and then use thinking to evaluate the result. Feeling is often not part of the picture.

For Eights, thinking is the Center of Intelligence that supports doing. Although they process information with the combination of doing and thinking, their orientation is to their own actions. Combining the logic and cleverness of the Thinking Center with an Eight's limitless energy produces extremely capable tacticians. If you happen to find yourself on the wrong side of an Eight, you will have a formidable opponent. Every move they make is well thought-out and calculated. Eights are very sure of themselves because they have complete trust in their own instincts and abilities.

Eights are also focused on the bottom-line. In her meetings with David and Marilyn, Elizabeth is always insisting that they look at results and know how everything they do will contribute to their goals. That's hard for David, who is always planning the next thing, and Marilyn, who is often concerned with how it will look to their members. But Elizabeth is upfront and seldom measures her words. Some have said she is blunt and tactless and often too firm. But from her perspective, there is much to be done, and wasting time with niceties and small talk limits what can be accomplished in a day.

Repressed feelings cause Eights to dismiss the importance of emotions and relationships. Using only two of the three centers means Eights often respond mechanically to life by intentionally doing the things that are important to them and ignoring things that are not. They can look like they have included the Feeling Center, when in reality they are using expressiveness and intensity, along with discussing common interests, to masquerade as an emotional connection in a relationship. It would be very unlikely, and awkward at best, if others tried to establish an emotional connection with Eights over coffee or in a small group. However, it is possible to connect with Eights in meaningful ways while building a Habitat for Humanity house or volunteering at a soup kitchen.

> Eights who are working to stay balanced in doing, thinking, and feeling are the most compassionate number on the Enneagram.

Eights are not aware of or concerned about their own feelings. As a result, they have no tolerance for people who want to continually talk about how they feel. When Eights start the work of bringing up the Feeling Center, they remain emotionally guarded. They have a tender side, but it is reserved for very few. If you have experienced their tenderness, you know that it represents feelings that are honest and pure.

KEYS FOR EIGHTS TO BRING UP FEELING

Eights can begin to increase their awareness by being conscious of the fact that the way the Centers of Intelligence interact in them fosters the compulsion to dominate, gain power, excite others, and make things move faster. Their focus is on doing, supported by thinking; feeling takes a back seat. That explains the difference between them and people who are in the other two stances. Eights need to meet others halfway—even if it feels like all the way. There is no other solution. My advice to Eights is to be aware when they are big in the room and sure they are right, and then compare that to when they are patient, curious, and more inclusive. Then ask: How is the outcome affected in each case? Does anything shift?

Because doing and thinking are so strongly linked, Eights need to learn to separate them and use each one independently. When doing is dominant, supported by thinking and in the absence of feeling, there is little, if any, awareness of collateral damage. People are often hurt by Eights because you act before you think. You can avoid that fragmentation by thinking before you act. It's the first step in learning to use all three centers.

Your passion is lust, and it informs your desire for influence, intensity, and control. Eights want to give everything they have, holding nothing back, and they are most at home in situations where the energy is high. Unfortunately, it's fairly easy to substitute lust for other emotions. Discernment will help you learn to recognize that you are repressing other feelings.

Though it is challenging for you to step back and make a choice to work toward balancing the three Centers of Intelligence, it is key to increasing your awareness. You will have to use the center you least favor, and that will reorder your priorities. If you choose balance, you will have more to offer than you could imagine, and you will be an asset in making a way for other aggressive numbers.

IT'S WORTH IT: JEN'S STORY

Being feeling repressed for me as an Eight has meant that feelings either appear to be absent or are overpowering and uncontrolled. Often when I'm telling a story, my voice will crack as if I run into the wall of emotional protection that I have carefully constructed over time. This crack, this break in the action, can lead to a flood of feelings that are overwhelming. It's like an explosion of unexpected emotions that come out of me all at once, leaving me feeling vulnerable and raw. And it feels terrible.

I'm a single adult who is content not being partnered, so I have to intentionally engage in practicing vulnerability with others. I am part of a community of friends who have all agreed that we will seek to be more open, more honest, and therefore more vulnerable with one another. During the past year we have stayed in conversations when unexpected feelings erupted, and we had the courage to speak truth into that messy space. They have helped me to give voice and words and wisdom to feelings and experiences that I have carried in my body for decades but had never been able to name. With compassion and love we have created holy space for one another.

TRY THIS

SOME TRANSFORMATIVE POSSIBILITIES

- Think about this: you hate being controlled. When your Enneagram personality is in charge, that's exactly what's happening. If you aren't managing your personality, you can be sure it is managing you.

- Be careful when you observe a power vacuum and find that you are inclined to step in to fill the void. Even if you save the day, you will not be rewarded for your choice. Consider that it perhaps is your role to set the stage for someone else to temporarily move into the leadership role.

- Be aware when you feel vulnerable because you quickly translate that feeling into boredom. Once the translation occurs, excess becomes the antidote (excess work, food, drink, partying, shopping, etc.).

■ Tap into your power to inspire other people:

- Make a list of people who have inspired you. Think about the qualities they have that you would like to emulate.

- Think about times when others have thanked you for being an inspiration to them. Then ask yourself if the Feeling Center was involved.

■ Consider that if you work to bring up the Feeling Center, it will help you in receiving affection from others.

■ Observe how your attention migrates to the natural, habitual places. Ask: Is there another way to look at this? Then take full advantage of the option to redirect your attention.

■ Keep in mind that those who are attracted to you because of your power do not love you for yourself, nor do you have affection for them. Remember that it's hard in Western culture to avoid the temptation to overvalue power.

■ Give some thought to some positive things that could happen if you loosened your control in work, family, and community. Be kind to yourself and practice it in ways and places that you feel safe. But practice.

QUESTIONS TO PONDER

What fear are you avoiding when you continue to resist slowing down and engaging with a contemplative practice?

When you are absolutely sure you are right, there is a good chance you're wrong.

Do you ever impose your ideas of justice on other people?

What would happen if you were willing to yield to others occasionally?

I've not met many Eights who know how deeply they are held in the hearts of others. I suspect there's a chance people don't tell them because they think they know. Eights who are working to stay balanced in doing, thinking, and feeling are the most compassionate number on the Enneagram. I think it's because they are passionate and just, and they understand how hard it is for some people to accommodate vulnerability.

Henri Nouwen wrote an article years ago titled "Compassion: Not Without Confrontation." And even though he was a self-identified Two, I think he must have learned this important point when he was in stress and in Eight. He wrote:

> We cannot suffer with the poor when we are unwilling to confront those persons and systems that cause poverty. We cannot set the captives free when we do not want to confront those who carry the keys. We cannot profess our solidarity with those who are oppressed when we are unwilling to confront the oppressor. Compassion without confrontation fades quickly to fruitless sentimental commiseration.

Eights intuitively know and practice what Nouwen suggests. And they do so with more grace and little collateral damage when they embrace the gift of feeling from their security number (Two), in order to include compassion in the ways they confront situations that are unjust.

CHAPTER SIX

THE DEPENDENT STANCE

MOVING TOWARD OTHERS

Every nonprofit I'm familiar with or have worked with, including Life in the Trinity Ministry, is held together with good leadership and an appropriate number of committed volunteers. Volunteers do so much of the day-to-day work that keeps us humming along as we all try to do good in the world. The trick in having volunteers work well together (and with the staff) while avoiding the pitfalls that can happen when people of different personalities collaborate is to recognize and understand how each one sees the world and how they respond.

One of our core groups happens to have three wonderful people who are all in the Dependent Stance. That means they all repress thinking, although that doesn't mean they don't think. Cindy, who is a One on the Enneagram, is a key part of the everyday operation of the Micah Center. She is there every time we have an event, making sure all the details are handled correctly. Since we all know the Enneagram, we understand that she is constantly seeking perfection in whatever she does and in all aspects of our work. We also understand that we have to allow her to do that by seeing her suggestions and criticisms as her attempt to help the rest of us to do better. It's not that she thinks we're not doing a good job but that we could always make improvements.

If we welcome Cindy's efforts rather than resisting them and understand that her criticisms are based on what she thinks is right and good,

she'll be engaged and productive. But if we don't allow the necessary
room for her to improve what she can, it hurts her feelings because her
doing as a One is supported by feelings. And when her feelings are hurt,
she sometimes digs in her heels. She is inclined to resist change and wants
to hold on to all that has already been enhanced as she sees fit. But the
wisdom of the Enneagram has changed that dynamic. She has become
aware that others neither see nor think the way she does. And more
importantly, she has learned to bring up her repressed thinking as a way
of making room for difference.

Mike is another core volunteer who has been a part of our work for
thirty-five years. As a Two, he needs to be needed. And he always has
been. Mike is responsible for the overall maintenance of the building. He
does all of the shopping for food and cleaning supplies, he makes the
prayer beads, and he handles setup and takedown for every meeting or
event. Before each event, he comes in to sweep the floors, clean the tables,
and check the snack supply for the following day. And he insists on coming
early each morning of an event to make coffee and bring fresh donuts for
the participants, along with a special breakfast basket for the speakers. A
year or so ago, he moved farther away from the Micah Center, but he still
wants to be the one to do all of the things he has always done even though
it means driving twenty-five minutes in dense Dallas traffic.

Cindy, thinking to save Mike from what she sees as an unnecessary
commute, suggests (and pretty much insists) that he doesn't need to make
all those drives. It seems to her and others that Mike could save himself
the commute by cleaning up at the end of the day and that they could
happily handle his morning routine. But that's not what Mike thinks.
In fact, he doesn't think. He feels hurt. In trying to be helpful and con-
siderate, Cindy and the staff are not mindful of Mike's need to encounter
and engage with the people who are finishing up the day when he ar-
rives in the evening and gathering for the day the next morning. Sensing
and meeting others' needs is as important to Mike as doing her very best

is to Cindy. To Mike their suggestion makes it seem as if they are not allowing him to be helpful and generous with his giving and enjoy the relationships that are so life-giving to him as a Two.

The growing edge for Mike, as part of our community, is not limited to allowing us to do what he does. He wants to do those jobs in part because he likes being with us and with the people who attend the conferences. The growth opportunity for him is to recognize that while he thinks he has few needs, and is therefore independent, his greatest need is to be needed. Naming that is one of the many steps toward

> The Dependent Stance, Ones, Twos, and Sixes, is made up of numbers who repress thinking while relying on feeling and doing. Their reference point is outside themselves—that's what makes them dependent.

embracing interdependence in relationships with the other volunteers, allowing them to take care of him on occasion. Receiving is awkward for Twos, and it's a challenge for him to practice by letting us help with his responsibilities at times, especially when he has other things that require his attention.

Lindsay, the third member of the team, has been a volunteer for several years, and she still volunteers but she is also on staff part time. She is an introvert, but she is also strong and smart and willing to speak up. Like all Sixes, she methodically goes about doing her work, unless her attention is drawn to something that she finds curious or disconcerting. In those times, she asks questions. The Enneagram has shown us that the way we can respond that shows honor and respect is allowing space for her questions, comments, and concerns. Thank God she is scanning the horizon for what could be misconstrued or go wrong within our ministry. She has saved us many times as we are all trying to work together in making the world a better place.

The questions that Lindsay asks can be very challenging (as is true for most Sixes), so much so that it sometimes makes the rest of the volunteers and staff a little bit uncomfortable. We might believe she is being alarmist when there's nothing to be concerned about, but the Enneagram has taught us to remember that Sixes are both thinking dominant and thinking repressed. That means Lindsay takes in information with the Thinking Center, then uses feeling and doing to make sense of things. Whatever thinking she is doing might not be productive—there may indeed be nothing to worry about—and she often knows it, so she may not trust her thinking. We need to be patient with her as she tries to be mindful, remembering that she may not intuitively use productive thinking in making choices and decisions. Like Cindy and Mike, Lindsay will have to choose to make her thinking intentional.

> **Perhaps the biggest challenge for those in the Dependent Stance is that they give away their power and get their sense of who they are from other people.**

Cindy has to recognize that not everyone sees opportunities for perfection where she does. Mike has to see that he is truly needed and valued for everything he does without exhausting himself to do it. And Lindsay needs to learn to recognize when her thinking is just habitual responses to her ongoing fear and anxiety. With awareness and intentionality all three can make their thinking—and their work together as volunteers— more productive.

THE THREE REALITIES OF REPRESSED THINKING

The Dependent Stance, Ones, Twos, and Sixes, is made up of numbers who repress thinking while relying on feeling and doing. Their reference point is outside themselves—that's what makes them dependent.

For Ones, doing is dominant and feeling supports doing, meaning they take in information using the Doing Center and then make sense of it by using both doing and feeling.

For Twos, feeling is dominant and doing supports feeling, meaning they take in information using the Feeling Center and then make sense of it by using both feeling and doing.

As one of the core numbers on the Enneagram, Sixes are both thinking dominant and thinking repressed. That means that they take in information from the environment using thinking (their dominant Center of Intelligence, as defined by their triad), but they don't use that center to make sense of or decide what to do with the information they have received. As a result, either doing or feeling will dominate the way Sixes make sense of things. One will lead and the other will support.

THE DEPENDENT STANCE

NUMBER	TRIAD	STANCE	PREFERRED AND DOMINANT CENTER	SUPPORT CENTER	REPRESSED CENTER
One	Gut	Dependent	Doing	Feeling	Thinking
Two	Heart	Dependent	Feeling	Doing	Thinking
Six	Head	Dependent	Thinking	Feeling / Doing Doing / Feeling	Thinking

The reality that Ones, Twos, and Sixes are thinking repressed doesn't mean they can't think. In fact, they insist that they think all the time. The question is what are they thinking about. Ones have an inner critic that talks constantly about everything. They get caught in silently arguing with that voice in an effort to defend themselves. To a One, this internal dialogue definitely feels like thinking.

Twos also believe they are thinking all the time. The problem is that the majority of the time they're thinking about relationships. That's nonproductive in its own way because Twos make up many of the scenarios they're thinking about, including all that require consideration and possibly action.

Along with the other Dependent numbers, Sixes argue that they never stop thinking. It's true. They are in the Head Triad, so they use thinking to take in information. But much of their thinking is unproductive because it is focused on what they fear and their compulsion to plan for the worst thing that could possibly happen—which seldom comes to pass. The imbalance of too much thinking without productive feeling and doing is exhausting for all three types.

The orientation to time for the Dependent Stance is the present.

I would suggest that there is a lack of equality in the three stances. When those who are doing repressed don't handle their responsibilities and get things done, people know it. They get reminders, and lectures too, and they don't get away with not doing. And we all recognize people who are feeling repressed. They are reminded from childhood on that they need to be more demonstrative with their emotions. But it's harder to discern when thinking is repressed. Those of us who make up this stance can get by for a long time on doing and feeling, especially because we believe we are thinking.

Along with the numbers in the other stances, Ones, Twos, and Sixes are somewhat offended when they first learn that they are primarily using only two of the three Centers of Intelligence. When the Thinking Center is underdeveloped, it makes it too easy to assimilate ideas from others and from the culture. The people who make up this stance can continue to make decisions based on opinions and belief systems that haven't been reexamined in years.

Ones, Twos, and Sixes consciously and unconsciously look at situations to evaluate what should be done and whether or not they are the ones to do it. They feel responsible for making all things within their purview better, so the immediate situation determines their agendas. They set very high standards for themselves, believing they have to do what others expect, and they have to do it well. Ones tend to pay attention to what needs to be done now. Twos are concerned with the needs of the person right in front of them. And Sixes are focused on their daily responsibilities and schedules.

It's very difficult for all three types to make a plan and stick to it because everything depends on what the day and people will ask of them. For the numbers in this stance, the day never seems long enough, and their to-do list is seldom completed. Ones do their work and then often redo what others have failed to do properly. Twos are overcommitted. And most Sixes find it difficult to appropriately gauge how much time a task will require.

Those in the Dependent Stance have a lot of trouble with boundaries. They don't know how to set boundaries for their time. They say yes to things that are not theirs to do, but for different reasons: Ones choose to say yes so things will be done correctly. Twos say yes so they can feel valued and needed. And Sixes say yes because they're team players who are almost always willing to be helpful.

All three numbers have trouble staying in their lane, and they're often offended by people who have good boundaries. Ones can even be offended when others with strong boundaries do not appreciate their advice for how things "should" be done. And Twos struggle to appreciate that boundaries in others are not rejection and not personal. Counterphobic Sixes accept boundaries in other people more graciously than phobic Sixes, Ones, and Twos because they have some boundaries of their own. But phobic Sixes are unaware of how much they violate others' boundaries while maintaining their own. (We see this when phobic Sixes ask lots of questions that they would not want others to ask them.)

These personality types struggle with evaluating situations objectively. They don't know how to evaluate their own performance from day to day, and they aren't objective about planning their lives, all because they only use two of the three Centers of Intelligence. Just using those two can seem adequate, but that's an illusion that may take time and effort to understand. Only the people closest to Ones, Twos, and Sixes would come to the conclusion that they are thinking repressed. Instead, they generally are known for being thoughtful, generous, and kind.

The orientation to time for the Dependent Stance is the present. This means that they're tethered to what's happening now. However, they have an added challenge in that all three struggle with anxiety, which they try to disguise—even to themselves—by being gracious and busy. In his book *Consolations*, David Whyte's challenge that we hold the past, the present, and the future all at the same time sounds somewhat familiar to Ones, Twos, and Sixes—not necessarily because they are mature enough to hold them appropriately and all at the same time, but because as Dependent numbers lacking boundaries, they easily adapt to the time orientation of the person whose needs they are addressing.

When I was a child, we made paper chains for the Christmas tree by cutting strips of construction paper and then gluing them in interlocking circles. This is like what Twos and Sixes do with fears and memories, past hurts and disappointments: when they experience a new hurt or disappointment they connect it to similar ones in their lives, which further increases their fear and anxiety. For example, if they fear that you are going to leave the relationship, they chain that feeling to everything (with you and with anyone else) that has happened in their lives to make them fear abandonment. And sometimes relationships collapse from the weight of this chaining. Only if Twos and Sixes use thinking to learn to identify this pattern can they stop doing it. It's really hard, but it's worth the work.

Ones are also prone to chaining, but it generally has to do with feelings that they are inherently bad or that they will be characterized as a failure. They respond by connecting what's happening in the present to perceived or real failures from the past, and that starts the pattern of chaining. The inner critic is particularly insistent when Ones are feeling inferior. Unless they can interrupt the chaining, they almost immediately take on behavior from the low side of Four. Ones find it difficult to manage the voice of the inner detractor and the weight of the chain.

Perhaps the biggest challenge for those in the Dependent Stance is that they give away their power and get their sense of who they are from other people. One of the goals for all three numbers must be to learn to know themselves from the inside out, rather than from the outside in, and to bring up productive thinking to help them do that.

1s

"AND IT WAS GOOD"

Ones like Cindy at the Micah Center see and interpret the world through doing. They have a consistent need to act on what seems correct or good or right, and they struggle to understand others who settle for less. They don't necessarily like being called the "Perfectionist" as they often are in Enneagram writings, yet they constantly search for perfection in thought, word, and deed. That's a big job! Along with action, they value determination, and the combination of these two informs their view of the world that suggests life is all about responsibility and work.

Ones struggle with a terrible, primal feeling of not being worthy or not being good enough, so they desperately try to be right. Because of this strong desire, they have an amazing ability to assess the potential for improvement in any situation. This is what Cindy is always doing for us. And she is willing to make sacrifices for what should be done, and that is certainly commendable. But there are two sides to everything, and the downside to a One's level of commitment is their expectation that others will be equally dedicated.

Comparison informs how Ones see the world. They mentally compare themselves to others and they judge those who don't try as hard as they do. Unfortunately, resentment often follows, as it has for Mike and Lindsay when Cindy seems relentless in her pursuit of perfection.

For Ones, the support Center of Intelligence is feeling. So although they take in information with doing, they make sense of it using both doing and feeling. Ones have intense feelings about what they do and how they do it. As a result, there isn't much feeling energy left for relationships. Ones feel good about what they do well. But when things don't turn out as they believe they should, Ones spiral into negative feelings. Self-blame leads to self-justification, which leads to blaming others, and the final result, again, is resentment.

Along with the other numbers in the Dependent Stance, Ones are unable to use thinking to appropriately evaluate themselves or the work they do. Nothing is ever good enough, so they just try harder and recommit to giving their best all the time, which is reinforced by their inner critic. We all have self-talk, but it doesn't compare to the One's experience. I can't imagine what it must be like to have a voice in my head that constantly tells me that what I do is wrong or inadequate at best. That condemning chatter is part of what Ones hear throughout every day of their lives. They respond by trying to evaluate their experience with overanalyzing and overthinking, both of which are a misuse of the Thinking Center.

Without the Enneagram, Ones seem to look for ways to prove that they are indeed flawed in some serious and irreparable ways. If they use Enneagram wisdom to learn to bring up thinking for its own purpose, in addition to using feeling and doing, Ones can find self-acceptance, self-respect, and peace. The inner critic can be recognized and quieted. And if any number on the Enneagram deserves peace, Ones do.

KEYS FOR ONES TO BRING UP THINKING

If you can separate the Doing and Feeling Centers, you will find there is more room for creativity and experimentation because you will be less emotionally attached to what you do. And that will create space for some soul work, not the perfect kind you believe you should pursue, but the growing edge that can be messy but rewarding. Once doing and feeling are functioning separately, you will have more confidence in decisions about what to do. It has been my observation that when Ones are able to clearly distinguish the different functions in each of the three centers, they find some time for activities other than work.

> For Ones, the support Center of Intelligence is feeling. So although they take in information with doing, they make sense of it using both doing and feeling. Comparison informs how Ones see the world.

Self-observation is essential for anyone in building awareness, but especially for Ones. Try imagining that you can hover above yourself, perhaps like a drone, just observing and re-cording information. The goal is to observe yourself nonjudgmentally, and that will be your biggest challenge. But it's necessary because when you judge yourself, which you do all day every day, you defend yourself. And that pattern is guaranteed to make your personality bigger. But the goal is to rightsize your personality so there will be more room for who you are underneath all of that to emerge.

You have a tendency as a One to notice everything that is wrong or should be done differently, like the crooked picture that hangs too close to the window and doesn't have nonglare glass. Or the place in the corner of the ceiling where someone used primer to cover a stain but never painted over it. You find it astonishing that men would wear a shirt with a button-down collar and button only one side. And the thought that someone would arrange their books by the color of the binding rather than in alphabetical order according to the author makes no sense at all. Changing this way of seeing will be a long, disciplined journey, but it will also be worth it because what you focus on determines what you miss. And you are missing so much.

Your passion is anger and it's usually triggered by imperfection. You turn that anger on yourself first, which means when it is expressed toward others it will be resentment. Resentment is much harder to handle than anger, and it hurts people in ways that are hard to forget. Oscar Ichazo, an early founding teacher of the Enneagram, taught that "anger is standing against reality." You can't win in a battle against reality.

And the reality is that perfection, if it could ever be achieved, is like an ice sculpture: it only lasts until something in the environment changes. For Ones who see imperfection everywhere, accepting that even if perfection is achieved it can't last, will free up some space for you to begin to think differently. And that work will help you discern what is—and is not—yours to pursue.

When you are being driven by your number and by its passion, you're not free. Our brothers and sisters of First Nations teach us that imperfection is necessary because it makes room for the Great Spirit. Their kind of thinking is worth your consideration.

IT'S WORTH IT: GEORJEAN'S STORY

I knew I was a One the first time I heard Suzanne describe them (me!). But the idea that I was thinking repressed did not ring true for me; in fact, it was offensive. Me, thinking repressed? Never! I have three degrees, something I wear proudly, dare I say arrogantly. After all, I am the first one in my family to go to college. Surely I'm a thinker. The more I processed and observed my behavior, the clearer it became to me that my thinking was almost always about what I needed to do or what others should do. I had detailed plans, I was accomplishing a lot, and I was thinking all the time. But it was almost always about doing, which is my dominant center.

Slowly but surely I have begun to own that my thinking is under-developed, and I have started to work on it. But it is hard. I often find that when I sit to prepare for a contemplative prayer time, I am thinking. My first thought is, what is wrong with the room? How it could be improved? What do I need to do to make this time and this space better? When I pick up my journal, I think about whether or not it's pretty. Are the lines on the paper spaced right? Does the cover feel good, and do I have the "perfect" writing instrument? As my awareness of all of that has increased, I am better, most days, at letting it go. It is the practice of letting go that has helped me most in managing my doing dominance. In fact, letting go may be the most important part of the whole process. I call it developing my "letting-go muscle." The more I practice, the more I am able to have space and time between when something happens and when I react. I have space to stop, breathe, and wait until something shifts, and then I can include thinking with my doing and feeling. It's a process—more of a spiral than a line, but most days I'm making progress.

TRY THIS

SOME TRANSFORMATIVE POSSIBILITIES

■ Notice when you are feeling impatient. It is an indication that you are judging others for not doing things the way you would do things. Or it might be that you are giving in to the inner critic's message that you are not good enough. As you begin to achieve some balance in the three centers, you will be more patient. The more balance, the more patience.

- Be aware that your idea of perfection is just that: *your* idea of perfection. Someone else's will surely be different from yours, and you can never be sure that you are right.

- Allow for the possibility that your unreachable standards cause resentment in you and in others.

- Think about that the next time you feel like you have to do more than seems necessary for the outcome to be right and good. I know, and respect, that you believe every step of a task should be done correctly. But perhaps a shortcut here and there would be okay. Some things are good enough. Perhaps not perfect, but good enough.

- Find a way, your way, to appreciate rather than judge lifestyles, people, religions, values, and beliefs that are different from yours. Learn to value people who are different from you. There's no shortcut with this one. You'll need to spend some time getting to know them.

- Try reading authors who you disagree with. Try to understand what they think, why they think as they do, and why they believe what they believe. They can't just be wrong. What might be an alternative explanation?

- Learn to ask "open, honest questions," a teaching from Parker J. Palmer: questions that are open ended and cannot be answered with yes or no, and questions you don't know the answer to. This will be a really great practice for you because Ones need to learn and accept that there is more than one right answer for everything.

- Plan something fun with someone you care about at least once a month. Life is not only about work and responsibility.

- Commit to practices that cultivate a quiet mind as a way of dealing with the reality that your inner critic will be with you always. Centering prayer is the best option. Using prayer beads is another because it requires doing, feeling, and thinking all at the same time.
- Consider finding both a therapist and a spiritual director. I've never met anyone who couldn't benefit from both.
- Try journaling. If it is to be a good experience for you, you will need to choose someone you trust who will promise to dispose of your journals should anything happen to you.
- Be kind to yourself. I know it is so difficult when you are dealing with your inner critic. Try giving him or her a name. And then call it out frequently in refuting the things you hear that make you feel less than. Be careful in your naming choice because it will need to last forever.

QUESTIONS TO PONDER

Do you believe your anger at imperfection and injustice makes you a good person?

What is it costing you to hold on to resentments? It's hard to let go of them, but it's even harder to keep them.

What would improve in your life if you put some well-defined boundaries around working at your job and at home?

Have you ever explored why you resist change? Is it fear? Would changing something in your life be an admission that it was wrong for some reason? Is there a chance that change would be life-giving?

Could you consider finding space in your life at least once a week when you can stop and rest? Maybe the tradeoff of doing everything perfectly for some peace and relaxation would be worth trying out.

You are so very generous with your time, and your commitment to doing things well is admirable. There is no doubt that your work ethic has made and will continue to make the world a better place. That won't change significantly if you choose to take more time for sitting and pondering and dreaming in place of some of the perfecting you are inclined to do.

Above all, remember that you are God's beloved just as you are. There is nothing you can do to get God to love you more, or less, than God loves you right now.

2s

WHAT DO I NEED?

Twos see and interpret the world through the Feeling Center. They are the most sensitive of all the numbers in part because they feel other people's feelings. They read people with uncanny accuracy and respond by trying to find ways to be helpful. And they usually are. They intuitively know how to respond to others because they are warm and relational without thinking about it. Our volunteer Mike always seems to know just what I need when I'm offering a workshop, whether it's a treat to start the day or a Coke with crushed ice in the afternoon, or even a hug when I'm feeling tired.

For Twos the support Center of Intelligence is doing. So although they take in information with feeling, they make sense of it using both feeling and doing. It is hard to imagine a better combination of unbalanced centers on the Enneagram. Twos can feel and do, and then celebrate what they've done, only to pick up on another feeling from yet another person and repeat the pattern. This is a tricky combination because it is so gratifying and has the potential to be very unhealthy. Twos don't stop to consider whether the doing is really helping the other person or if it is good for them to neglect their own needs. Mike was so attached to coming in early and late, despite a punishing commute, that he ended up not just tired but also at times not as gracious as usual.

The image Twos project is one of generosity, kindness, and availability. And while their desire is pure, like all of us, their motives are often somewhat self-serving. Their giving is fueled by a need to be needed because Twos can't imagine that you would want them if you don't need them, and their heart's desire is to be wanted. The problem is there is an unspoken assumption that others will sense and meet their needs in return. Twos give until they're empty and then they reconnect to their own lives with nothing left for themselves. Their response is hurt and anger when they feel used and taken for granted. They may also encourage more relationships than they can manage. Their capacity for connecting with other people exceeds the amount of time they have for other people, and is sometimes costly in the relationships with those they love the most.

Since thinking is repressed, Twos don't adequately question whether or not their immediate responses are appropriate. They don't stick to schedules, and personal goals get lost because they are responding to whoever they're trying to help. Essentially, Twos have terrible boundaries. They don't know where they end and where other people begin, and as a result they find it difficult to be objective in deciding how to respond to daily life. They like following their feelings, and other people like their caring response, so Twos seldom question the need for thinking.

The Enneagram consistently highlights our weaknesses, but not without naming the strengths we have for more enlightened choices. For Twos, when every feeling is demanding a response from the Doing Center, much of what is in their best interest is set aside or ignored. However, when Twos do the work to balance the three centers, thinking makes it possible for them to identify what is, and what is not, theirs to do.

KEYS FOR TWOS TO BRING UP THINKING

The initial requirement for finding and achieving balance using the three Centers of Intelligence is awareness. Twos are easily distracted when challenged to practice self-observation because their point of reference is outside of themselves. They know themselves by how other people respond to them, or to their work, or to an invitation to connect in some way. Only by paying attention to what they feel and then what they do will they be able to use thinking to evaluate whether that is appropriate. It is only when they've engaged thinking as well that they can be objective and truly in contact with reality.

It is noteworthy that this pattern of feeling first and responding with "What can I do?" knows no limits. Twos can have very strong feelings about something they hear on the news or someone they've never met and wonder what they can do. The answer is often nothing—there is nothing you can do. But that doesn't negate the desire. The path to acceptance and then peace is bringing up repressed thinking to realize these kinds of limits.

The passion for Twos is pride. Don Riso and Russ Hudson have defined Enneagram pride as "the inability or unwillingness to acknowledge one's own needs and suffering, while tending to the needs of someone else." In a Two, pride could sound like "I'm the best giver you've ever met, and I don't need much, so I can just help you." When you think you don't have needs, it makes you seem somewhat superior to anyone who does (and you can hardly tolerate neediness in yourself). So it is key that you admit to and name your own needs.

The most difficult questions I'm ever asked as a Two are *What are you feeling?* and *What do you need?* My response was always, "I don't have any idea." I've worked really hard to be able to answer these two questions, and my life is better when I can. Even so, answering these questions is still uncomfortable.

So I would offer two things for your consideration. First, I've discovered I was afraid that if I asked for what I needed but didn't receive it, I wouldn't be able to handle it. I was wrong. It's complicated, but I can deal with it. (It's actually much harder for me to know what I'm feeling.) Second, overuse of an intuitive way of knowing, in reading and serving the needs and desires of other people, while helping us make our way in the world, can be costly. When I am habitually reading and responding to the feelings of others, my own feelings become even more obscured. Twos will have to do the work of naming and claiming our own feelings if we want to experience mutuality in relationships with people we love.

> For Twos the support Center of Intelligence is doing. So although they take in information with feeling, they make sense of it using both feeling and doing.

IT'S WORTH IT: DEBRA'S STORY

A few years ago, I decided that I could no longer live the way I was living. As I talked to friends and began doing stance work, I realized that I was showing up in my relationships as codependent and needy, nowhere close to who I truly am. In order to balance my centers, I had to commit to bring up thinking instead of acting automatically. Every day I ask myself, "What is mine and mine alone to do today?" and "Have I been honoring the reality of my resources (time, money, energy, emotions)?" I have to consistently define what my needs are and answer truthfully.

It's been incredibly hard, but I no longer go searching for relationships or friendships to define me or give me worth. I am the only one responsible for my choices, continued healing, and self-forgiveness, and now I am finally comfortable in my own skin. No one else is responsible for meeting my needs.

TRY THIS

SOME TRANSFORMATIVE POSSIBILITIES

■ Be intentional about bringing up thinking because you don't make any intuitive moves on the Enneagram that give you access to thinking. Your wings are in (One), doing, and in (Three), feeling. In stress you go to (Eight), doing. In security you go to (Four), feeling.

■ Spend time alone. If there is even one other person in the room, your attention will be focused on that person. In quiet time alone you will have a chance to observe how you use or misuse the Thinking Center.

■ Pay attention to what you think about. Then pay attention to how you respond to your thoughts. Some things you could do:

   • Don't respond immediately to people or situations.

   • Have a schedule for your day and honor it.

   • Communicate your needs when you know them directly, not indirectly.

   • Find ways to screen your phone calls, emails, and texts.

   • Practice saying no to requests.

■ Cultivate productive, more objective thinking by developing it with reading nonfiction on topics that interest you. Try to resist memoirs, biographies, and novels because they keep you trapped in responding to feelings—it's satisfying but not helpful for growth.

■ Be aware when you are suddenly interested in things you've never been interested in before, like a certain kind of music, science, fly fishing, poetry, or world history. Ask yourself why you're interested. If it's because someone you want to know better has those interests, you can be sure your personality is in charge.

- Work at creating boundaries. If we don't, how will we ever learn to recognize and respect someone else's?

- Make a list of what you lose when you shift into being the person you think others want you to be. It is only by letting go of your need to make everyone like you that you can respect and value the person that you are.

- Stop and rest and take care of yourself. It's not commendable if you're tired from doing good in the world.

- Learn to listen to your body. This may be challenging because most Twos don't like their bodies. Your head will lie to you, and your heart will lie to you, but your body will not. So, anything you can do to reengage with your physical self will ultimately be a gift.

- Use a contemplative practice to bring up the Thinking Center. As a Two, centering prayer has been the most helpful to me in my effort to manage my Feeling Center while trying to bring up repressed thinking. A daily "sit" has added a rhythm to my life that I can't imagine living without.

QUESTIONS TO PONDER

Are you afraid that if you don't take care of others, you are unlovable?

Do you lose touch with who you are by trying to make people like you? You might try asking yourself this question once or twice a day: Do I try to make people like me by being less like me?

What is yours to do? You may want to use the following questions that have helped me in my practice. As I consider connecting with someone—whether face to face or with a text or a phone call—I ask myself these questions:

■ *Why am I moving toward this person?*

■ *What if anything do I expect to get in return?*

■ *Does this person want my help?*

Your generosity toward others is unparalleled. It's my hope that you will learn over time to be as generous with yourself.

6s

ALL SHALL BE WELL

For Sixes, thinking is both preferred and repressed. This means they see and interpret the world through the Thinking Center, but often they don't use thinking productively to process or make sense of the information they've received. Though they insist they are indeed thinking, the reality is that what they're thinking about can drag them off into various anxieties and fears, or mislead them to focus on things that don't matter. Their habitual patterns of thinking often don't help them make sense of their lives or the world around them.

Sixes are focused on information and analysis. They're curious about what's happening around them but then, because of repressed thinking, they question their own judgment or interpretation. They respond by gathering ideas from experts and people they know who are seemingly well-informed. Unfortunately, the responses they receive don't alleviate their desire for more information. To them, information is security, but it is often elusive. Lindsay, for example, may send the staff and other volunteers an email with six links to internet articles about some issue we're facing and then gets upset when we don't take it as seriously as she does.

Thinking is tricky for Sixes because they're constantly gathering data, but then they often have a hard time knowing what to do with it, mainly because they don't know if it's trustworthy. So they ask lots and lots of questions, often in the pursuit of security but not necessarily productively. Because for a Six, there are never enough answers. The questioning and equivocating can make other people impatient, so then Sixes stop participating (although they don't leave). Underlying all of this is the fact that because many Sixes don't trust themselves (and their thinking), that also makes it very difficult for them to trust other people.

It's important to keep in mind that there are two kinds of Sixes. Both are focused on the authorities who have expertise and thus power, but their responses are considerably different. Phobic Sixes believe if they follow the lead of authority figures in their lives, they will be safe. In a sense these authorities substitute for the Six's own productive thinking. Counterphobic Sixes don't trust people in authority until they prove themselves. They're determined to think independently until others have earned their confidence. It could be said that phobic Sixes are lazy thinkers and that counterphobic Sixes overthink and overanalyze. Both examples are the result of repressed thinking, again, because it's not productive.

> Because thinking is repressed, Sixes use doing and feeling to make sense out of life. The combination of these two centers is how we know Sixes.

Fear is the passion for Sixes. Richard Rohr said that "the passions can be understood as emergency solutions that were used in the early childhood development of a person as a way of coming to terms with his or her environment." But as we get older, our passion becomes the emergency itself. And that is true for Sixes and fear: they believe that if they are aware and if they prepare for everything that could go wrong, then they will be safe. But that can never be true—it is impossible to do so.

I think Sixes were actually prepared for the pandemic of 2020—they had plenty of food and supplies, including toilet paper—but not for the experience of being quarantined because they had no frame of reference to prepare for that. In reality we all experience fear in ways specific to our individual types. Sixes, because of their preferred thinking, believe information is important. But from the position of repressed thinking, they are never sure they have the right information or enough to quell their fear. Preferring and repressing thinking causes fear.

In Sixes, when fear takes a break, anxiety takes its place. Although we often use these two terms interchangeably, *anxiety* is concern about possible future events, but *fear* is in regard to things that are happening in real time. Phobic Sixes identify with their fear, and their solution is flight. Counterphobic Sixes are those who identify with countering their fear. Their choice is to fight.

Because their orientation to time is the present and everything seems to make equal demands on their attention, Sixes feel a need to schedule their time and organize the day. A plan alleviates some of their anxiety about getting everything done, even though they don't necessarily follow it. Until they've done some good personal work, the plan can easily be replaced depending on how the day unfolds and what other people ask of them. Sixes, along with every other number, allow their personalities to take the lead when they're tired or stressed or afraid. Our Enneagram numbers work when nothing else does, even when we don't know what our preferences are or understand our choices. When combined with repressed thinking, that means Sixes dutifully move from one thing to another without discerning whether that is still the appropriate course of action.

Because thinking is repressed, Sixes use doing and feeling to make sense out of life. The combination of these two centers is how we know Sixes. They complete to-do lists and projects and find it easy to connect with others through commonly shared experiences. All of this comes from the Doing Center. Feeling helps Sixes relate to other people, and it usually includes making connections. This probably explains why Sixes like belonging to groups more than any other number.

Sixes are the number on the Enneagram that is the most concerned about the common good. That is very likely connected to the fact that they take in information with thinking but then they use feeling and doing to respond. This is one of the best of the gifts that Sixes offer to the larger community. They aren't big in the room. While they are capable of leading, they don't necessarily need to. They want to be part of something that is bigger than they are. And Sixes are loyal beyond measure, but the downside of that is that the loyalty may go unexamined. People change and circumstances change, so loyalty should inform change but should not prevent it.

> Sixes are the number on the Enneagram that is the most concerned about the common good.

KEYS FOR SIXES TO BRING UP THINKING

Sixes need to develop an understanding of the difference between *habitual* thinking and *productive* thinking. As for all numbers, self-awareness is key. Sixes need to learn when they are simply asking questions and when they are making preparations for dire emergencies in response to fear or anxiety. You can only do that by paying attention to when your thoughts are whirling around your cares and worries. It's then that you can stop and ask yourself whether there is another way to deal with whatever is before you.

If you learn to distinguish between habitual thinking and productive thinking, it will significantly change how you make decisions for your life. It's not difficult to do, but sticking with it is. Consider these words of Danish philosopher Soren Kierkegaard: "Life can only be understood backwards, but it must be lived forwards." In the beginning you will find that you understand more of your thinking by looking back. That's okay. In time what you learn will have a positive effect on choices you make moving forward.

Doing and feeling need to be separated and each used for its own purpose. That will make you more productive with less motion. Aggressive numbers can't think their feelings. Withdrawing numbers can't think or have feelings about doing something and get it done. And Dependent numbers can't feel their thoughts.

IT'S WORTH IT: LESLIE'S STORY

When I first learned that Enneagram Sixes are in the Head Triad and have dominant thinking, it was like I felt seen for the first time. When I learned that Sixes are also repressed in their Thinking Center, it was like the feedback loop of my mind was given language.

For me, a thought starts with a level of energy, potential, and even hope. It then moves quickly down a path of what I don't want to happen, leaving me low, fearful, and anxious. Then another new thought comes, seeking to repair the lowness, only to end the same way and keeping the feedback loop in motion.

What helps me both manage my strength of mind and my repressed use of thoughts is to slow down the pace by breathing, moving my body (walking or stretching), and being curious about where my thoughts are going. I try to be gentle with myself and say things like, "This person I'm thinking about is important to me, so it makes sense that my fear would be to lose them. No wonder my thoughts are getting dark or scary. I feel vulnerable right now." Comforting myself can help slow me down. If I have access to this, I then ask myself, "What would I like to see happen?" This is such an awkward and difficult shift for me, but unless I do these balancing practices, my mind regularly goes to the worry.

As unfamiliar as peace and hope are for me, imagining a bright future of hopes fulfilled is so good for my mind and gives me a whole-brained worldview that offers me some levity and even joy.

TRY THIS

SOME TRANSFORMATIVE POSSIBILITIES

■ Make a list of your fears. Remember, you can't change what you can't name. After you compile the list, do some additional work with separating the fears from anxieties. For example, it is appropriate to be afraid of catching Covid-19, but worrying about whether the vaccine will work is an anxiety.

■ Instead of scanning for danger, try changing your focus and start looking for potential good and safety. What you focus on determines what you miss.

■ Work on reframing distorted thinking patterns and perceptions. They are generally the result of anxiety and projection. All dependent numbers make up things, but Ones and Twos are not as attached to their unproductive thinking as you are.

■ Learn to trust yourself the way other people do.

■ Limit preparation for what could happen by examining your concerns and selecting the things that are more likely to happen.

■ Learn to respect your capacity for being inner-directed and handling many things in life that are confusing, frightening, unfamiliar, or perhaps even traumatic. That is part of who you authentically are. Don't sell yourself short.

■ Make a plan for what you are willing to reveal about your life. Sometimes you say too much, and you share yourself with the wrong people. Sometimes you do the opposite and others believe you want to know about them, but you don't want them to know who you are.

■ Give yourself—and others—a break from all of the questions. You may find that the questions themselves have been the source of the ongoing apprehension you experience in your daily life. And make sure you don't already know the answer to the questions you ask.

■ Set aside time to be in silence. Dependent numbers don't have much appreciation for silence. I think it's because when we're quiet, we make up stuff, and we would rather keep busy than do the work to bring up productive thinking. Only in silence will you learn to trust your own impressions and thinking processes. When you're with other people, there's a good chance you value their thoughts over your own.

■ Consider committing to practicing contemplative prayer every day for six months. If you can "sit" at the same time each day, it will have added benefit. There is no better practice for those of us who are thinking repressed. This practice has the potential to teach when thinking is valuable and when it's a waste of time because the only thing you can do wrong is fail to show up.

■ Journal daily. It's a discipline, to be sure. But it will help you get to know yourself, and you will find out how wise you are. You know so much more than you give yourself credit for! You can get started by using my friend Hunter Mobley's prompt: "From this day I remember . . ."

QUESTIONS TO PONDER

What is at the root of your tendency to avoid the insecurity of change? Perhaps it's difficult for Sixes to imagine the result due to repressed thinking. Is that true for you?

Ask yourself these questions for a week or two when you have some time and space to increase your understanding of yourself:

- *Who are the people you most admire? Most dislike?*

- *What positive or negative qualities do they possess?*

- *What keeps you from seeing similar strengths and weaknesses in yourself?*

Are you keeping score and protecting yourself with chaining everything from the past to the present? I would encourage you to examine your thoughts and feelings about forgiveness. If you find them to be troubling, consider some therapy. What do you gain or lose by refusing to forgive past transgressions?

What if you used thinking productively to see how trusting yourself would make your life simpler, easier, and more pleasant? What would you have to give up to do that?

Your commitment to loyalty means you don't leave organizations when you don't get your way. You don't leave churches when the pastor makes changes that you wouldn't have chosen. You are loyal to the people in your communities, even when they behave badly. From an outside perspective, it appears that you honestly believe in the goodness of humanity. If you can find a way to teach others how you do that, the world will be a safer place. There are a lot of words that describe you, but *steadfastness* is not mentioned as often as I would like.

WHAT ARE YOU WILLING TO GIVE UP FOR TRANSFORMATION?

God is not found in the soul by adding anything, but by a process of subtraction.

MEISTER ECKHART

J oe and I take time for a spiritual retreat at least once a year. We choose a place that will be both quiet and comfortable. We hope for good weather, good food, and few distractions. And Joe always has a plan for our time away that will serve as a guide for our spiritual quest for the coming year. In 2011, we had a limited amount of time, so Joe planned for us to stay at a retreat house in San Antonio. After consulting with two of our spiritual wisdom advisors in planning the reading and spiritual practices we would commit to, they decided the theme for our retreat would be the Spirituality of Subtraction.

It's about a five-hour drive from Dallas to San Antonio and we didn't need to be there until late afternoon so we could settle in before dinner. Joe thought it would be a good idea for us to prepare for the retreat by listening while we were traveling to some recordings of Father Richard Rohr talking about the spiritual practice of simplicity, and I agreed.

Joe punched the button to start the cassette (remember, this was 2011), but I stopped it and said, "Hey, before we get started, would it be okay with you if we stop at one of the outlet malls on the way?" He wasn't excited about the idea, but he said, "I guess so. Why? Do we need something?"

And then I said, "Well, I'd like to go to one of the kitchen stores to look for a new toaster."

"I like our toaster. Why do we need a new one?"

"I'd like to have one of those new, wide-mouth toasters."

"Why?"

"Mostly for bagels. We can't toast bagels in ours, but we'll be able to if we get one of the new ones."

"We don't eat bagels."

"That's because we don't have a wide-mouth toaster!"

In his Nineness, Joe merged with my agenda and agreed. He started the cassette again and I took a few notes as we listened. Richard was saying things such as, "We are a people who don't seem to be able to even understand, much less be capable of, spiritual surrender." He talked about our preference for a spirituality of "holding on" and "taking" as opposed to "letting go" and "surrender."

As we listened, I was nodding in agreement and trying to write down the ideas that I wanted to remember. From time to time Joe would say, "That's brilliant! Did you hear that?"

As we approached the outlet mall, Joe took the exit, and we found a parking place right in front. Joe paused the cassette and we headed in to look for the toaster. On the way in I talked to him about the different kinds of spreads we could buy to put on toasted bagels, and even suggested that we could buy a variety of both on our way home.

We found the toaster almost immediately. They had one that had a special button for toasting bagels. I looked around a bit to see if there was anything else we might need for our kitchen. Aware that Joe was more than ready to leave, I quickly chose two new potholders—who doesn't need to replace potholders?—and put them on the counter. He finished the transaction, and we headed to the car.

I was chatting about bagels and cream cheese and potholders as we left the parking lot, and just as we turned to get on the highway, Joe punched play on the cassette. With God as my witness, Richard Rohr said, "It's just like all those people who think they have to go out and buy a wide-mouthed toaster. . ."

Joe turned and looked at me, his face covered with an expression of both satisfaction and justification. He didn't say anything, but he didn't have to. In that moment, and now as I write this, I'm aware that at times I am still grasping and needy, and honestly, I think I always will be.

Letting go is really hard.

There is a big difference between change and transformation. *Change* is when we take on something new. *Transformation* occurs when something old falls away, usually beyond our control.

I've gone on retreats and returned saying that I've changed. I've read books that "changed my life." After a good movie I've declared to Joe that "I will never be the same." I've heard sermons, listened to podcasts, taken classes, and read good articles in magazines that I then subscribed to, declaring that each one had changed me along the way. Maybe they did. But change is not transformation. The wisdom teachers I respect insist that all great spirituality is about letting go. And I believe that. And yet I find that I am inclined to *add* things to my life as part of my commitment of learning to let go. It sounds ridiculous, but I'd bet you might have done the same thing.

> There is a big difference between change and transformation.

The great challenge in seeking transformation is that we have no control over when transformative opportunities will come our way.

So, in seeking wholeness, we need to be aware and willing and open to allowing something new to happen. And we need to resist the temptation to believe we won't have to give up anything. We don't much like that. In fact, many of us are caught in the frenzy of our time and our culture, so we continue to add more and move faster and faster, looking for the kind of peace that we've heard about, the peace that surpasses our understanding.

If you're like me, having read this book there are lots of things here that you are hoping to *do* or *think* about, or perhaps you are inviting a group to gather with you to share feelings and some thoughts and ideas about the Enneagram and wholeness and balance.

But, to paraphrase a quote from E. L. Doctorow about the craft of writing, I would suggest that the journey that leads us toward spiritual transformation and wholeness is like driving at night in the fog. You can only see as far as the headlights, but you can make the whole trip that way.

It is my greatest hope that you are both excited and anxious to get to work and continue the journey. But it's our lifelong journey, and we will have to be patient as the path before us is illuminated, day by day. Without some awareness and intentionality, we will be adding rather than allowing, leading rather than following, and deciding rather than discerning.

There are many choices to be made, and we will have to be disciplined if we are to give each chosen practice time to affect how we see and respond to life. And we will have to reflect deeply on whether we are ready to be transformed, whether we will let go of what stands in our way.

Are you willing to give up the expectation of immediate gratification?

We will need to be kind to ourselves while we try to change some of our favorite and most comforting habits, having become aware that they lead us away from instead of toward a more balanced life.

Are you willing to give up the familiar for the unknown?

We will be challenged at times to say no to things our personalities would love to do, so we can say yes to things that will feed our souls.

Are you willing to say no in order to be able to say yes?

If you stick with this work, allowing personality to fall away while you seek to be more of who you truly are, it will very likely bring about some changes in your relationships. You may find out that some of the people you love and care about don't want you to change and grow. They like you just like you are.

Are you willing to give up the false peace in some of your relationships for inner peace for yourself?

It is really important, whether we are learning and growing with the Enneagram or yoga or contemplative prayer or any other spiritual or contemplative practice, that we remember this:

- Each heart must make its own choices.
- Each heart must have its own experience.
- Each experience has its own purpose.

Are you willing to offer to others the opportunity to freely choose their own way—to have their own experiences of life, learning, and growing as they do, while giving up your desire to have them see life through your lens and make decisions from your perspective?

I know that these are some of the questions that are key to transformation. And I know that they are hard and cannot be easily answered. In fact, they have to be answered over and over again. Every day, sometimes many times, I have to ask myself, "Suzanne, what are you willing to give up for transformation?" so that I can answer the hallmark question for my life: *What is mine to do?*

Transformation is a lifetime process, a process of letting go and staying with the inner work. I feel very fortunate to have found the Enneagram as a companion on this journey toward wholeness. It has given me so much—and I hope you will find its insights just as rich and helpful.

For me, the journey continues, as it will for you.

ACKNOWLEDGMENTS

When it comes to the Enneagram, my teachers are everywhere. They are in the classes I teach and the audience when I speak. They are in the airport when I travel, in our church when I worship, in the grocery store when I shop, and in my neighborhood when I come home. They are all the people who are making their way through the world doing the best they know how with what they have and how they see, and I owe them a great debt.

Most of all I want to thank my husband, Joseph Stabile. His unending commitment to me and our life together is both honoring and challenging as he continues to insist that we commit ourselves to the work we are called to. Our children and their husbands and wives, along with our grandchildren, are my motivation for wanting to do my part to make the world a better place. I am so grateful for all of them. Thank you, Joey, Billy, Will, Sam, Jenny, Cory, Noah, Elle, Piper, Joel, Whitney, Gracie, Joley, Jase, Josephine, BJ, and Devon for oh so much! Saying yes to writing this book meant saying no to you more often than I would ever want to.

Joel Stabile and Laura Addis, I cannot imagine trying to work in the world without the two of you. Your gifts are many, your work is exceptional, and your commitment and creativity help to sustain Life in the Trinity Ministry in want and in plenty.

Rob and Jean Estes, Tommy and Carrie Johnstone, Webb and Rose Estes, I don't know that we could have survived the pandemic without your generosity. We are forever grateful!

There are so many people who give their time and energy to the work of Life in the Trinity Ministry: Mike George, Joe's best friend for fifty-seven years, and his wife, Patsy; Lindsay O'Connor and Cindy Short, without you LTM could not be what it is. Carolyn Teel, my best friend for fifty-two years; Luci Neuman, B. C. and Karen Hosch, Dr. John and Stephanie Burk, Christine Min, John Brim, Tom Hoekstra, and Jane Henry.

Father Richard Rohr invited me into the study of this ancient wisdom, so whatever my teaching has become is easily traced back to him.

I want to acknowledge and express my thanks to those who have led the way for me as I have studied the Enneagram. Their insights make this wisdom more accessible for all of us: A. H. Almaas, Beatrice Chestnut, Thomas Condon, David Daniels, Theodorre Donson, Andres Ebert, Russ Hudson, Kathleen Hurley, Margaret Keyes, Dr. Jerome D. Lubbe, Sandra Maitri, Roxanne Howe-Murphy, Claudio Naranjo, Helen Palmer, Virginia Price, Susan Reynolds, Don Riso, Lynette Sheppard, Clarence Thompson, and Suzanne Zuercher OSB.

I am so grateful for my friend and literary agent, Sheryl Fullerton. She is, quite simply, the best of the best.

There are no words to adequately thank the men and women who have been in my apprentice program and cohorts for the past twelve years. They have taught me so much of what I know to be true about the Enneagram. I am grateful beyond measure for the thousands of people who have shared their weekends and their stories with me over the past thirty-three years. They are the reason the information I have gathered about the Enneagram became wisdom.

To Jeff Crosby, former publisher for InterVarsity Press, I respect you without reservation and I trust you in all things. Special thanks to Cindy Bunch, associate publisher and director of editorial at

InterVarsity Press. You continue to help me find my way in the world of writing and publishing. This book is better because of your flexibility, encouragement, and unending patience with me. The staff at IVP is a gathering of men and women who are smart, and creative, and so good at what they do—and above all, they are really good human beings. Thank you to the editorial team: Elissa Schauer, I'm so grateful for your trust in my ways of knowing and understanding the Enneagram and for the grace you extend to me; Allison Rieck, Ashley Davila, and Lisa Renninger. The interior design and layout reflect the vision and talent of Daniel van Loon. Thank you, David Fassett, for the beautiful cover. And to marketing, Lori Neff and Andrew Bronson, I'm so thankful for your commitment to making this book available to readers everywhere.

To Dr. Shirley Corbitt (posthumously) and Marge Buchanan, witnesses to all of my adult life and the first to tell me I should write. Dr. Bob Hughes, thank you for walking with our family for the past eighteen years.

I am, and have been, well loved by many people who encourage me to live my life well and to do what is mine to do regarding teaching the Enneagram. To each of you I am very grateful.

NOTES

INTRODUCTION: TOWARD A BALANCED LIFE

11 *As a flyer:* Henri J. M. Nouwen, *Our Greatest Gift: A Meditation on Dying and Caring* (New York: HarperCollins, 1995).

....

PART ONE

CHAPTER ONE: WHAT DO I FEEL?

35 *Emotions are not made:* Suzanne Zuercher, OSB, *Enneagram Spirituality: From Compulsion to Contemplation* (Notre Dame, IN: Ava Maria Press, 1992).

36 *To understand human nature:* Sam Sommers, *Situations Matter* (New York: Riverhead Books, 2011).

3s: I CAN ALLOW FEELINGS

48 *feeling wheel:* See www.gottman.com/blog/printable-feeling-wheel.

CHAPTER TWO: WHAT DO I THINK?

68 *Fear is the enemy:* James Hollis, PhD, *What Matters Most: Living a More Considered Life* (New York: Gotham Books, 2010), 13.

69 *We are accepted:* F. Forrester Church, ed., *The Essential Tillich* (Chicago: University of Chicago Press, 1987).

8s: I CAN SLOW DOWN

104 *constant need for intensity:* Don Richard Riso and Russ Hudson, *The Wisdom of the Enneagram* (New York: Bantam, 1999).

1s: TWO THINGS CAN BE TRUE

119 *in Ones the anger is repressed:* Don Richard Riso and Russ Hudson, *The Wisdom of the Enneagram* (New York: Bantam, 1999).

....

PART TWO

OVERVIEW: THE SOUL WORK OF THE REPRESSED CENTER

130 *An underdeveloped soul:* Kathy Hurley and Theodorre Donson, *Discover Your Soul Potential: Using the Enneagram to Awaken Spiritual Vitality* (Lakewood, CO: WindWalker Press, 2000).

130   *world of constant cares:* Hurley and Donson, *Discover Your Soul Potential.*

135   *dependent, aggressive, and withdrawing types:* Jerome Wagner, "Karen Horney's
       Three Trends (Moving Towards, Against, Away From) and the Enneagram
       Styles," https://enneagramspectrum.com/184/karen-horneys-three-trends
       -moving-towards-against-away-from-and-the-enneagram-styles.

CHAPTER FOUR: THE WITHDRAWING STANCE

142   *inhabit the past:* David Whyte, *Consolations: The Solace, Nourishment and
       Underlying Meaning of Everyday Words* (Langley, WA: Many Rivers Press,
       2015), 139.

9s: MAKE A CHOICE—YOU CAN CHANGE YOUR MIND

162   *It's not okay to assert yourself:* Don Richard Riso and Russ Hudson, *The
       Wisdom of the Enneagram* (New York: Bantam, 1999), 31.

8s: VULNERABILITY IS NOT WEAKNESS

195   *We cannot suffer with the poor:* Henri J. M. Nouwen in Henri J. M. Nouwen,
       Donald P. McNeill, and Douglas A. Morrison, *Compassion: A Reflection
       on the Christian Life* (Image/Doubleday: New York, 1982), 124.

CHAPTER SIX: THE DEPENDENT STANCE

204   *hold the past, the present:* David Whyte, *Consolations: The Solace, Nour-
       ishment and Underlying Meaning of Everyday Words* (Langley, WA: Many
       Rivers Press, 2015), 139.

1s: "AND IT WAS GOOD"

209   *anger is standing against reality:* Oscar Ichazo in Claudio Naranjo, MD,
       Ennea-type Structures: Self-Analysis for the Seeker (Nevada City, CA:
       Gateways), 21.

2s: WHAT DO I NEED?

216   *the inability or unwillingness:* Don Richard Riso and Russ Hudson, *The
       Wisdom of the Enneagram* (New York: Bantam, 1999), 23.

6s: ALL SHALL BE WELL

222   *passions can be understood:* Richard Rohr and Andreas Ebert, *The
       Enneagram: A Christian Perspective* (New York: Crossroad, 2001).

ALSO AVAILABLE

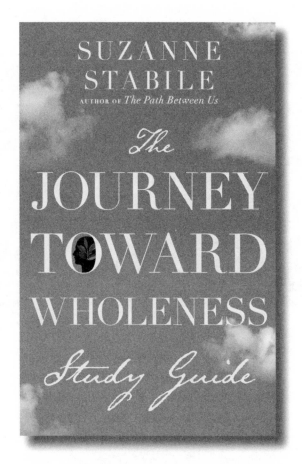

ALSO AVAILABLE

ALSO AVAILABLE

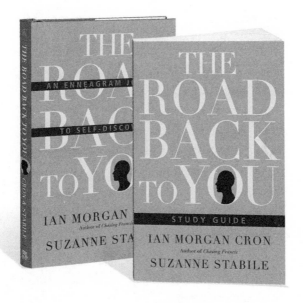

LIFE IN THE TRINITY
MINISTRY

Drawing on timeless wisdom and the Living Word, Life in the Trinity Ministry is a community serving the Triune God and our brothers and sisters through study dedicated to encouraging self-knowledge and fostering spiritual maturity.

What does the Lord require of you but to do justice, and to love kindness, and to walk humbly with your God? Micah 6:8

The Enneagram: Know Your Number
Suzanne Stabile

The Enneagram: Stress and Security
Suzanne Stabile

The Enneagram Journey Curriculum
and **Participant's Guide**
Suzanne Stabile

Centering Prayer
Reverend Joseph Stabile

LTM Cohort Program
Suzanne and Reverend Joseph Stabile

For more information about Suzanne or any of these resources, go to lifeinthetrinityministry.com.

BECOMING OUR TRUE SELVES

The nautilus is one of the sea's oldest creatures. Beginning with a tight center, its remarkable growth pattern can be seen in the ever-enlarging chambers that spiral outward. The nautilus in the IVP Formatio logo symbolizes deep inward work of spiritual formation that begins rooted in our souls and then opens to the world as we experience spiritual transformation. The shell takes on a stunning pearlized appearance as it ages and forms in much the same way as the souls of those who devote themselves to spiritual practice. Formatio books draw on the ancient wisdom of the saints and the early church as well as the rich resources of Scripture, applying tradition to the needs of contemporary life and practice.

Within each of us is a longing to be in God's presence. Formatio books call us into our deepest desires and help us to become our true selves in the light of God's grace.

VISIT
ivpress.com/formatio
*to see all of the books in the
line and to sign up for the
IVP Formatio newsletter.*